One Woman's War

"The Work carried out by the WAAF on Radar Operations
during WW2 was a major contribution in the defence of our
country. This book is a testament to their valuable work."
Dame Vera Lynn

Reviews

"Brilliantly written and eminently readable, the title *One Woman's War* belies the amazing and rare wartime career path of Eileen Le Croissette in the Women's Auxiliary Air Force. This is no ordinary story; to become a Filterer Officer required great aptitude, skill and judgement to interpret the often-confusing information from the Radar stations.

Altogether there were probably less than 200 WAAF Filterer Officers and Eileen was one of only eight to serve in Belgium targeting the V2 missile launch sites. As well as serving at 11 Group Filter room, Fighter Command on the night of the Normandy invasion, she later received the *Big Ben* warning when the first V2 was detected approaching London.

Married only a few weeks, Eileen was then posted to 33 Wing, 2nd Tactical Air Force in Belgium, as a carefully chosen team sent to locate mobile V2 launch sites, by Radar and sound data, so airborne strikes could destroy the launchers before they returned to base. As war ends, she is assigned as a guide to the German concentration camp near Brussels. Not only facing the stark reminders of torture and human degradation, she suffered insults and antagonism from the imprisoned Belgian collaborators who replaced the camp inmates.

The whole story is set against an intriguing backdrop of family and long-time friendships and correspondence with German and French pen pals, which in retrospect, contained many different perspectives on the Nazi regime."
Squadron Leader Mike S. Dean MBE (Historical Radar Archive)

"The Few could not have won the Battle of Britain if it had not been for the Many. Eileen Younghusband vividly reveals the unsung heroism of Fighter Command's Filter Room during the Second World War. One Woman's War is living, breathing history, resonant with warmth and personality."
Jed Mercurio (Writer – The Legend of the Tamworth Two, The Grimleys, Cardiac Arrest)

"In her autobiography, *Not an Ordinary Life*, Eileen Younghusband gave us a glimpse into the wartime experiences of a WAAF Special Duties Officer engaged in vital work in the Filter Rooms of Fighter Command, and later, in Belgium helping to track the deadly V-2 rockets back to their firing sites. In *One Woman's War*, this vital period in the life of this country, is described in considerable detail, and constitutes an important personal account of an aspect of women's contribution to the Allied victory in 1945 that is often overlooked or not known about at all. The work that went on in the Filter Room was crucial to the ultimate success of Fighter Command operations during the Battle of Britain, demanding the highest level of concentration and competence from the women engaged in it.

This personal account also provides a fascinating insight into the creation and operation of the Chain Home defence system and the wartime development of Radar, written by one who was among the first to have to get to grips with this unprecedented leap forward in wartime technology. The view from the Filter Room' shows us the progress of the war in Europe in a new light, and the book also tells a very human story of how momentous events shaped the life of a young woman in wartime Britain."

Stephen Walton (Senior Curator Documents and Sound Section, Imperial War Museum, Duxford)

"This is a remarkable memoir. A personal story intimately entwined with the great events of the Second World War. As a naïve teenage exchange student, Eileen Younghusband saw Nazi Germany in the months before war broke out. Returning on the eve of war she later took a crucial role in the British Radar operations. Then, venturing abroad again, she saw firsthand the post war desolation of Europe. This is a story of great events – but it is also the story of how those great events shaped and transformed the life of a young London office worker."

Nick Skinner (BBC Wales)

The right of Eileen Younghusband to be identified as the Author of the Work has been asserted by her in accordance with the Copyright, Designs and Patents Act 1988.

©Eileen Younghusband 2011

ISBN 978-0-9566826-2-8

Published by
Candy Jar Books Ltd.
113-116 Bute Street, Cardiff
Bay, CF10 5EQ
www.candy-jar.co.uk

Printed and bound by
CPI Antony Rowe
Chippenham, Wiltshire, UK

A catalogue record of this
book is available from the
British Library

Set in Calisto MT 11 / 20

Dedication

This book is dedicated to the airwomen and officers of the Women's Auxiliary Air Force who worked in the Filter Rooms of RAF Fighter Command during World War Two. The Filter Room was the nerve centre of the Radar chain. These young women working underground, at speed, both night and day, calculated from Radar reports the position, height and numbers of all aircraft approaching our coast. From this information, hostile aircraft were intercepted, air raid warnings given and air sea rescue undertaken. They remained silent under the Official Secrets Act for thirty years. The story of their work has never been told. It is time to recognise their invaluable contribution to the successful defence of Great Britain in its darkest hour.

Acknowledgements

It is thanks to the encouragement of Hugh Turnbull that this book has been written. After his interview with me entitled *My Secret War* for BBC Radio Wales, he suggested I should write in detail the unknown story of the Filter Rooms of RAF Fighter Command, which were the key to the victory in the Battle of Britain, and also of the V2 attacks on South East England and on Antwerp, the Allies first free port. He has acted as editor, researcher and encourager.

My thanks must also go to Flight Officer Grogono (now Joan Arundel) for her memories of the Filter Room at the outbreak of World War Two.

I am grateful for the support I have received from Shaun Russell and Justin Chaloner from my publisher Candy Jar Books and the assistance given to me by Lino and Dorothy Scaglioni of Isis Printing Ltd.

I thank Jill Le Croissette for her perceptive comments on the text. I give a special thanks to Dame Vera Lynn for her encouragement and also to Emma Soames for graciously contributing a foreword. I appreciate too the comments of those who have reviewed the book.

The pictures of the Filter Room are taken from the IWM film entitled *The Scope and Purpose of the Filter Room*, reference AMY01 and 02 and are used by courtesy of the Imperial War Museum.

CONTENTS

FOREWORD

If, like me you come from the generation below that of Eileen Younghusband, most of your knowledge about the conduct of the aerial defence of the realm, as practised by young women during the Second World War, will have been gleaned from those marvellous black and white movies that showed smart young WAAF in the Operations Rooms pushing counters across a board. But theirs is only a part of the story. Told here for the first time is the tale of the Filterers and Plotters who translated the raw mathematical information coming from RDF (Radar) into intelligible and usable data, then passed on to the Operations Rooms. It was a vitally important role and one which demanded mathematical knowledge, speed and hastily gathered experience gleaned from short training and then many hundreds of shifts – many of them through the long nights in cold bunkers underground.

Although the girls in the Operations Rooms are famous from those movies, the WAAF working behind them had an even greater weight of responsibility on their young shoulders. This is the first record of their work and Younghusband's account of events such as the Baedeker bombings bring this difficult and previously unacknowledged work vividly to life. It is excellent to be reminded what a great debt we owe to this group of brave, dedicated young women who, in a highly charged and stressful situation where time was of the essence did so much to save our country from destruction.

There is much that is remarkable about Eileen Younghusband: she is 90 years old and is as sharp as a knife – indeed I suspect that she is a lot brighter than many half her age. Her intelligence is supplemented by an extraordinary memory which certainly serves her well in these pages. Her recounting of the war is extraordinary in its detail and reads as freshly as if it all happened a couple of years ago. It also explains the technicalities of how

Radar worked then in accessible language. We should be thankful not only for Younghusband's skill and the role she played then, but for her prodigious memory and energy that has produced this interesting volume.

As a grandchild of Sir Winston Churchill, I have a particular interest in her war experiences. She plotted one of Churchill's flights when he was travelling back to Britain in an unidentified aircraft from a visit to Roosevelt in Washington. Towards the end of the war, after several promotions she ended up as an Officer at the most significant station, Stanmore which was responsible for the defence of London from incoming aerial attack. Here she saw my grandfather again.

One Woman's War adds to the war archive that becomes increasingly important as the participants in the 1939-45 war gradually age and pass away, many of them taking their memories with them. As well as producing this readable account of her years in uniform, Eileen Younghusband has brought an extraordinary period and a previously unrecorded part of our air defences to life.

Emma Soames
Editor-at-large, SAGA Magazine.

Prologue

The Forgotten Letter

It fell out of the back of the book I was reading – a book of classic French poetry I hadn't opened for years. Thinking back, it must have been around 1940 when I bought it – or did I have it as a gift? I just can't remember but it must have been over seventy years since it last left my bookshelves. And now a bit of my past had dropped from its pages. I picked up the letter – it was written on a small piece of faded blue notepaper, torn at the edges. The writing was faint. As I read the words, I realised it wasn't really a letter, more a statement or perhaps a message.

It was headed: *On Saying Goodbye.* The writing was small, neat, a man's hand I felt sure! It went on: *"Twenty-four hours from now and all the goodbyes will have been said. Goodbye – what an expression! It is said with such a variety of feelings.*

"The goodbye you just let fall after a casual meeting in a pub or after a few hours journey on a train. Goodbye has no real meaning then – it's just the thing to say and people expect it.

"Then there's the goodbye you say at the end of a long period at a school, or on a camp when posted. It brings a feeling of sorrow for a few hours as one realises that you are leaving behind friends you've made, associations you will miss; but not for long, for as new associations are formed, the old ones are soon forgotten."

As I turned over the page, my mind was searching back into my memory. Could I remember who had written this, what piece of my past had I turned up after all these years? I felt foolish, old. Surely this must have meant something to me once. I continued reading...

"Now the real goodbye is different. And the one I say today will be that. It will convey all the meaning of the other goodbyes and much more. The word will be the same but the feeling will be so much deeper. I have no illusions as to whether we will meet again, but in the forming of new associations there is one I shall never forget – I just can't. So to me this goodbye will mean more than the mere act of parting. To quote Lamartine again: 'Une seule être me manquera et le monde sera dépeuplé' – One sole person I will miss and the world will seem empty."

And that was the finish, no signature, no other clue.

I lay back in my chair. The book fell to the floor. I began thinking, feverishly concentrating on those years at the beginning of the war. I was 18 and working in the centre of London for a firm of paper agents. It wasn't a big office and there were only a few employees. Daily we would make the journey up to town from the suburbs during the Blitz. Each morning some familiar building would be missing – bombed or burned out during the night. Each day the journey became more hazardous, land mines hanging from telegraph lines as you passed in the train, warnings of unexploded bombs.

Gradually the faces formed in my mind of the other people working with me in the office; older men who belonged to the Territorial Army and who were soon called up, those nearing retirement who gradually accepted more work to make up for those who had already gone, and then the younger men who waited each day to volunteer or to be conscripted. It was these young men who joined me for lunch on the Embankment, eating our sandwiches or sometimes taking a beer and a snack in the

2

nearby pub. I had forgotten them completely over the years, and yet at that time of danger, of apprehension, we used to talk about everything – our desires and our despair, our innermost thoughts and our fears. We were all idealists, our aims and hopes for the future so defined.

We thought we knew each other so very well. And as my mind went back to those times, a face was gradually forming in my memory. There was a young man, half-Jewish, dark, intense, an intellectual and a loner, who would attach himself to me. We would read poetry and discuss important things with the wisdom – or dogged ignorance – of youth. Yes, we had had an association, not a love affair but a joining of minds. Inevitably he had been called up into the Army, roughing it with the rest, training on damp, cold campsites. No books there to read, only the rough male company in the NAAFI.

He was right, we never did meet again. I think perhaps I heard them say in the office that he had gone abroad, in the infantry. And then I heard he was missing – after that, nothing. A few weeks later, I left the office and I moved away. Then just last night, as I read this letter, his life touched mine one more time.

Au Pair

War was not on my mind on that day in May 1938. Aged almost seventeen, I was preparing to travel alone to France, to spend six months teaching three French children to speak English. I was looking forward to an exciting change in my life.

Having left school almost immediately after my sixteenth birthday, I had started working in the City of London at the Head Office of the Scottish Provident Institution, a long-established life assurance company. It was a safe but uninspiring office job in the cash department. I very soon realised how male-dominated the City was, and I could see little chance of a great future for a young woman without a university education.

I was delighted when the former German teacher at my grammar school contacted my parents to find out whether I would be interested in joining his newly-formed company, the School Travel Service. He saw the potential for organising school exchanges with France and Germany, since these languages were being taught in all grammar schools. He knew that I had shown considerable aptitude in learning both French and German, and he was suggesting that I could work for him and be trained to plan future educational tours for parties of schoolchildren to visit various European countries, a comparatively new experience in the 1930s.

He insisted that it would be necessary for me to spend a period of time in both France and Germany to polish up my language skills. He suggested I should apply for an au pair position.

He explained: 'As an au pair, you will live as a member of the family and you will teach the children English. You will no doubt have the evening meal with the family. They will pay all your expenses and give you some pocket money. Don't expect much. But it will be an excellent way of improving your French.' As an au pair in those days, conditions were vastly different from what they are now. You were not expected to do any housework.

I was sure I would enjoy the challenge and my parents were keen to encourage me, as they knew I had always enjoyed meeting the overseas students my music teacher entertained each summer. I think too they realised I was sensible and could cope with travelling alone. So we set about trying to find a suitable French family.

A reputable and much-valued source of advertisements for such a position was the magazine *The Lady*. The very first copy we bought contained a request from a Madame Boucher. The advertisement said she was looking for a young woman to teach her children good English. The person chosen would live as part of the family, who spent the summer at Contrexeville in Alsace, and returned to Paris for the winter months. Full references must be provided.

I composed a letter in French with a copy in English, together with suitable references from my potential employer Victor Groves, the minister of the local Baptist Church and my previous headmaster. I anxiously awaited a reply. It was not long in coming. Almost by return of post, I received a letter from the family inviting me to join them as soon as possible and saying they would send both train and boat tickets.

The letter was signed Marcel Boucher and was written on notepaper headed Chambre des Députés, Paris. To my great surprise I found my future home would be with the family of a French Member of Parliament. He gave his address as Le Val, Contrexeville, in the Departement des Vosges, Alsace.

Consulting the atlas and a travel guide, I found the town of Contrexeville was in the Vosges Mountains near Vittel and was a famous spa town renowned for its health-giving waters. I also noticed that it was near the frontier with Germany. This fact did not concern me particularly as at that time I knew little about international affairs and the politics of Europe.

I occasionally read my parents' newspaper, the *News Chronicle,* and I regularly listened to the radio. Even the *Anschluss* of Austria by Hitler, when his troops marched in and occupied that country, did not seem to concern our government unduly. Britain wanted peace at any cost and was pursuing a policy of appeasement. The troubles in the Sudentenland of Czechoslovakia with its mostly German-speaking population were not discussed openly. All these happenings seemed so remote and hardly likely to impinge on my young life.

At that time, I had two German pen friends. Werner Eisner from Berlin always wrote in German. He never mentioned the politics of his country but only wrote about his studies to be a dentist and his love of music and literature. He had written that he would have to do his six months *Arbeitsdienst,* which he described as work service that all young men had to do.

The other pen friend was a girl from Hamburg, Hanneliese Nelb, known as Hali. She wrote in English and in every letter told me how wonderful Hitler was and how he was going to get rid of all the Jews. Even this didn't mean much to me. At school we never knew or were interested in people's religion and I had no idea whether anyone I knew was Jewish.

I immediately gave in my notice to the Scottish Provident Institution who said they were sorry to lose me. I was happy to go. No more early morning struggles to find a seat on a crowded London and North Eastern train, no more having a quick sandwich on a bench outside the Royal Exchange, and no more having to wear a scratchy maroon overall in the front office when all the men were wearing smart suits and ties. I bought a few extra clothes and a new suitcase and took £5, a fortune in those days to me, from my post office account. I was ready for this exciting new adventure.

The boat train to the Channel coast and the crossing to Calais went according to plan. In May there were hardly any holiday travellers. Britain was still coming out of the Great Depression of the early Thirties and few people had the money to take holidays abroad. I remember being anxious not to lose my luggage and holding on to it tightly throughout the journey.

On arrival in France, I found my French was understood enough to get me from the harbour to the railway station. I knew I would have to change trains in Paris but all went well and soon I was on my last stage of the journey. I was the only single young passenger to dismount from the train at my final destination and was easily recognised. An elegant lady, dressed in the height of fashion, approached me and asked if I was '*la jeune fille anglaise?*'

'*Oui, Madame,*' I replied. She escorted me through the ticket control and out into the street. There was a large black Mercedes waiting, complete with uniformed chauffeur. My luggage was put in the boot and Madame and I sat in the back of the car. I was tired after the journey and barely noticed the scenery as we passed, but I remember thinking the town looked attractive with its many parks filled with spring flowers.

Madame did not speak much to me during the journey; I think she was weighing me up. Fortunately, she did seem to understand my fractured French. I am sure she was as glad about that as I was! Before long we stopped at the entrance of a large house. It looked like a mansion to me. There was a long drive through a tree-lined avenue. The front door was flanked by carved pillars. This was *Le Val*, my home for the next six months.

It dawned on me that my life would be very different from now on. I was somewhat apprehensive and wondered how I would cope with these new and opulent surroundings. How would I manage at meal times? Did they eat the same way that we did? Were my clothes suitable? We entered through the large wrought iron gates into a beautiful garden surrounded with trees.

As we walked up to the house, the door was opened by a servant. A tall distinguished-looking gentleman came forward to greet me. He was a handsome imposing man and seemed charming. He shook my hand and said *'Bienvenue chez nous'*. I tried to relax. Madame showed me to my room on the first floor – it was large and sunny, overlooking the garden. The furniture was massive and ornately decorated with ormolu. My small collection of clothes was lost in the wardrobe.

Madame had suggested I should come down when I was ready and take *gouter* with the children. This was the name for the five o'clock snack the children had, and consisted of weak tea without milk, and tartines, small portions of baguettes buttered and filled with jam. But no English cakes!

Around twenty minutes later, somewhat refreshed having washed and changed out of my travelling clothes, I returned downstairs. The children were waiting for me. They were a little shy at first but within a short time I was chatting with them and being understood. The eldest boy, Francois, said a few words in English to welcome me and then quickly changed back to French.

Francois was eleven, his younger brother Jean just nine, and their little sister, Hélène, five. They were attractive children, beautifully behaved and very friendly. They grabbed me by the hand and took me off to their quarters – separate bedrooms for each of them and a study. They were anxious to show me their toys and books and where we would do our studying together. I was beginning to feel at home.

Within a few days I slipped into a regular routine. I would join the children for breakfast, typically French, consisting of large mugs of coffee, freshly baked croissants and fruit. We would try to talk in English. They had so far very little knowledge of the language. Hélène, although the youngest, was soon saying a few words with quite a good accent. Jean was less courageous and remained silent unless I spoke to him directly and made him answer. Francois, being the oldest, worked hard, knowing that it would be useful to him in his future studies.

At nine o'clock they went for their main lessons, which were held in a specially built school room. There were two live-in tutors, a rather elderly and very strict German woman, Frau Gertrud, who taught German and Mathematics, and a younger French teacher, Mademoiselle Ginette, who taught the other subjects, French Grammar and Literature, History, Geography and Art. They lived in an apartment above the garage and had their meals there. I rarely met them. They seemed to live a separate life from the household.

It was a beautiful summer. Every weekday afternoon I would give the children a formal lesson in English grammar followed by a little reading and conversation. This would last for an hour and a half and then we would go outside into the grounds of the house and play games, speaking in English as much as possible. They enjoyed Robin Hood – making bows and arrows from the branches of trees – and sometimes playing Hide and Seek in the beautiful grounds around their home. After the inevitable *gouter* at five o'clock, most evenings the children and I would go to the town swimming pool.

I learnt soon after my arrival that their father, in addition to being the representative for the area in the French Parliament in Paris, had been the mayor of Contrexeville for many years and was a much-respected figure in the town. During his tenure he had managed to make the spa resort known worldwide and its mineral waters became famous. The town had prospered. So when the children went to swim, the pool was closed to outsiders and they had it completely to themselves. If we didn't swim they would go to the golf course for private lessons. Their life was very privileged but I never can remember them mixing with other children. They did not seem to have any friends.

The family usually spent from May to August at Contrexeville but returned to Paris in the autumn and winter. There was no doubt that they were very rich and influential. It seems Madame Boucher belonged to the family who owned La Tremoille, a famous hotel in Paris. I was looking forward to the move to the capital later in the year but life in Contrexeville was never boring.

In the mornings I was able to visit the town or walk in the beautiful countryside close to the house. I would often amble down to the thermal centre and taste the waters from the fountain. I found it rather metallic. I noticed that the people who were staying in the centre were mostly middle-aged or older and appeared very prosperous. I could hear many German voices amongst them. When I went in the local shops, many people were speaking in the Alsace dialect, a mixture of French and German.

Each evening I dined with Madame and Monsieur and with any visitors they might have. Regularly there were important people visiting. I recall the Prime Minister of Romania spending several days there. I believe it was Octavian Goga, who was also a poet. He turned to me and said: *'Votre français est bien meilleur que le mien'*. I was flattered. We always spoke French during dinner and this was wonderful practice for me. The long dining table was elaborately set with an embroidered damask cloth, silver cutlery, elegant central silver candelabra, and daily the gardener would provide beautiful bowls of fresh flowers from the garden.

The meals were always superb. The cook, a middle-aged woman, spoke the local dialect but provided the most wonderful classic French dishes at every meal. I still remember the day she served a *Croquembouche* as the dessert. This famous dish consists of *petits choux* (cream puffs) built up to a pyramid with a caramelised sugar, on a decorated base of praline or nougat and topped with a special decoration, often a fleur-de-lys. The finest wines were offered but sadly I was at that time a confirmed teetotaller. I often think now of the wonderful wines I might have tasted.

The time passed swiftly. June and July came and went. During the latter part of August, Monsieur Boucher, who was an officer in the French Army reserve, rejoined his regiment, *Les Chasseurs,* part of the Artillery. I thought it was his annual camp. I had no idea where this was taking place. Meanwhile life went on at the house as usual. I had no opportunity to see a newspaper and had not heard the radio, so I knew nothing of what was going on in the outside world.

We were living in our own little universe. I was enjoying life in this lovely French home and was learning so much about the French way of life. I found teaching the children enjoyable. Their English was improving daily and I was very proud of them. Then came the phone call.

It was about six o'clock in the evening a few days after Monsieur Boucher had left. Madame called me into her private room. She looked very serious. I wondered what I had done. It was then she told me the news. Her husband had been called up. His regiment was camped on the west side of the River Rhine near Strasbourg. On the other side was Germany.

I had not realised that despite being forbidden to do so, Hitler had been moving his troops into the demilitarised zone of the Rhineland, which included that part of Alsace Lorraine that Germany had retained after the First World War. They were now massing on the far side of the Rhine and were mining the river. More troops were arriving daily. The build-up was ominous. Monsieur Boucher had phoned to say he was very worried. He thought Hitler was preparing to invade France and another war was about to start.

Madame told me that her husband considered it too dangerous for me to remain there as the invasion could take place any moment and I could be cut off, unable to return home. She had instructions to arrange for me to return at once. I was told to pack my things immediately and be ready to leave early the next day. I was shocked and stood there speechless. All my plans for the future seemed in jeopardy. What would I do now? Madame could see that I was upset but she suggested that the first thing I should do was to go and explain to the children that I had to leave for my own safety.

When I joined them and told them the news, they could not understand why. I said that it might be dangerous for me to stay but I did not mention the possibility of war to them. They were already very upset. Little Hélène ran to me crying and hugged me saying: *'Don't go, Mademoiselle, don't go'*. I turned away so they could not see me crying too, and went to my room and started to pack my few belongings. Then I phoned my family, who knew a little more of what had been happening in Germany than I did and had been anxiously listening to the daily news. We did not realise it but this was the build up to the Munich crisis.

Early the next morning I was handed tickets for the train to Calais via Paris and for the ferry to Dover. The cook gave me a small packet with a freshly baked baguette, some cheese and fruit for the journey. I was driven to the station and the children said a sad goodbye. The train was packed with travellers, all apparently anxious to get away from the German border with Alsace. The journey was slow, stopping at every station and picking up more and more people. The carriages were crammed with bodies and luggage. Everyone looked serious and they were talking in undertones. Finally we reached Paris.

I made my way to the Gare du Nord but I found it was too late for me to make my connection. I realised I would have to find somewhere to stay the night. I had very little money on me and I didn't know Paris at all. I walked the streets looking for a cheap hotel, getting more and more anxious. Finally, I found a gendarme and asked for his help. He was very kind and took me to a *Centre d'Accueil* in Boulevard Raspail. This was a rest centre run by a religious order.

The gendarme asked the nun in charge if she could help. I was lucky; she said she had room for me. I was shown to a curtained area off a large dormitory. In this small space was a bed, a chair, a small bedside table and a Bible. By now it was fairly late in the evening and I was very tired. Thankfully I lay down on the bed and soon was fast asleep. The first part of my journey home was over.

I rose early the next day. After a typical French breakfast of hot croissants and jam and a large bowl of coffee, I paid for my stay. It cost five old francs, almost all the money I had left. Then once again I made for the Gare du Nord and a train to Calais.

I remember the journey vividly. Every seat seemed to be taken. Thankfully, I found one empty in the last compartment. Everyone was talking in German. I soon realised my fellow travellers were Jews escaping from Hitler's Germany. They had masses of belongings in suitcases, in bags or tied up in sheets. They seemed frightened. I remembered then the words of my German pen friend Hali and how she told me that Hitler was going to get rid of all the Jews.

The train sped on through the French countryside. As we neared Calais, my companions seemed to relax a little. They began to open their luggage and take out pieces of jewellery and put them on. They even began to smile. I think they knew they were going to get to England and to safety. After a calm crossing in the ferry, I made my way to North London and home. I wondered what I would do now – whether war was imminent and how it would affect all our lives.

The Munich Crisis

It was late August. I had been home only a few days but everything felt different. People seemed nervous. The experiences of the past few weeks had changed me considerably. I had grown up.

My father's work at the furniture factory had changed. They were now engaged on government contracts. He would not talk about it. My mother too now worked in the office there. I would listen avidly to the BBC news bulletins and read details of Hitler's every move in the newspaper.

I had to find a job. I could not hang around at home doing nothing. I did not think it would be too difficult. I had a good commercial training; shorthand, typing, knowledge of accounts and sure enough, within a week, I was employed again, this time locally. I became secretary to the managing director of a company making lipstick cases, not the most interesting of posts but at least I was earning some money to contribute to the family finances. My brother was still at school.

Every day the news became more disturbing. The Sudetenland of Czechoslovakia was Hitler's next target. He demanded that this border area, populated mostly by ethnic Germans, be ceded to Germany. Czechoslovakia had military alliances with France and the Soviet Union. How would they react? The situation could escalate into war. The British Prime

Minister, Neville Chamberlain, still pursuing his policy of appeasement, decided that negotiating directly with Hitler could defuse the crisis. Amongst the Government there was a feeling that Germany had been treated unfairly in the provisions of the Treaty of Versailles in 1918.

It had become increasingly obvious that the requirements of this treaty were no longer being respected. Germany had been re-arming for some time and had moved troops into the demilitarised zones of the Rhineland. Hitler had by this time annexed Austria with little apparent response from the rest of Europe and had used the Spanish Civil War as an opportunity to give the bomber pilots of his air force, the Luftwaffe, valuable operational experience. It was these squadrons of German bombers that had caused the carnage of Guernica in Northern Spain.

Chamberlain, seeing his vision of peace ebbing away, requested a meeting with Hitler. This was held early in September at Berchtesgaden. Hitler would not compromise on the Sudetenland, insisting it should be absorbed into Germany, threatening he would go to war if refused. He talked about the *persecuted Germans* living in this borderland and suggested it should simply be handed over to Germany. Chamberlain, anxious to pacify Hitler, agreed to consider asking the Czechs to do this but would not give a definite answer without getting his government's approval. On his return, the British Government was persuaded to agree to Hitler's demands.

On September 19th the Czech Government was told to hand over all territory on the border with Germany where there was a majority of the German-speaking population. That country had no say in the matter and was not allowed to be present at the meeting. Realising they had been abandoned by their Western allies; the Czechs gave in and agreed the terms. The British public was either unaware of the significance of these decisions or had not considered the possible consequences.

A subsequent meeting was held in Munich between Chamberlain, the French Premier Daladier and Hitler, with Mussolini, the Italian Fascist leader, also present. There the infamous Munich treaty was signed, with Chamberlain agreeing a further demand that all non-Germans would be removed from the Sudetenland. On September 30th, the four leaders signed the Munich Agreement allowing the German Army to occupy the Sudetenland the following day. Chamberlain returned to Britain where he made his famous speech proclaiming 'Peace in our time.'

We all believed him and were lured into a false sense of security. We continued with our day-to-day lives, relieved. Meanwhile Germany continued to re-arm. I still received frequent letters from my two German pen friends. Werner told me he was being called up to do his *Arbeitsdienst,* the six-month work service all young German men had to do. He said he would be building *Autobahnen,* the new big trunk roads, criss-crossing Germany. His medical training had been completed and he was now a qualified dentist. This physical work on the roads must have been a very different way of life for him. Hali wrote proudly informing me she had joined the *Hitlerjugend,* the military youth movement. My life went on uneventfully.

I was in contact again with my school boyfriend, George, who had moved to Staines where his father was the Inspector of Police. He told me he had joined the Territorial Army and was a keen member of the local rowing club. We were able to meet occasionally and were becoming more than just friends. George was a Scot and proud of it, often teasing me and calling me '*Sassenach.*' He was blond-haired, very good looking and six feet tall – my friends called him a good catch! The Southgate County Old Scholars Hockey Club was flourishing and I played each weekend in their first eleven. Life seemed to be safe again.

However, the new job I was now doing was not working out. I was increasingly unhappy there. Although the director I worked for had initially seemed charming, as time went by his attitude changed. He started becoming unpleasantly familiar. He would put his arm around me and make sexual innuendos. He was a man in his late forties, rather tubby and married with a small family. I was seventeen-years-old and not sure how to handle this situation. Finally I said I wanted to leave. It was not a happy time working out my month's notice. He made things extremely unpleasant for me. Nowadays I suppose I would have made a lot more fuss and asked for compensation, citing sexual harassment, but that did not happen then.

I obtained a new post very quickly and joined Corke Sons and Company Ltd of New Bridge Street, close to St. Paul's Cathedral and Fleet Street. I was travelling daily once more to the City of London. This company acted as agents for various papermaking companies. They sold all types of paper, newsprint, bond writing paper and speciality papers for packaging gifts and confectionery. They had contacts with factories in Finland, Germany and France as well as Britain. Once more I was travelling on the London North Eastern Railway in crowded carriages, but now people were talking more, discussing politics and especially Germany.

ONE WOMAN'S WAR

It was a friendly office and we enjoyed our lunchtimes together when we would discuss every subject under the sun. I was happy working there. I became particularly friendly with one young man. We both wrote poetry and would often talk about our favourite poets and compare our own amateur efforts. We were young and very introspective. Today I cannot remember his name but I can remember his face. He had a sensitive look, quiet and reflective. I often wonder what happened to him in the coming years. Did he survive?

Christmas came and we celebrated a little more than usual, thinking that peace was secured. The Finnish paper company sent all the staff a box of lager as a present. I struggled home on the train with this heavy load, together with other presents from my colleagues. Being teetotal then, due to my strict Baptist upbringing, the lager was passed on to my grandfather who had always enjoyed his daily glass of beer down at the local pub. I was very popular with him that day.

The New Year dawned. It was 1939 and we were all convinced that the danger of war had receded. Czechoslovakia by then had been divided up. After Germany took over the Sudentenland, Poland and Hungary annexed Czech territory on their borders. The larger powers ignored these actions; appeasement at all costs was the order of the day. Behind the scenes, unknown to the public, belatedly the British Government was using the time gained by the pact with Hitler to build up our armed services' capabilities.

The British public had no idea the damaging effect the policy of appeasement had on our Army, Navy and Air Force. Neither did we realise how strong the German Wehrmacht had become. The work done by the young men on their *Arbeitsdienst* had built a

20

network of roads, shielded by avenues of trees, to provide cover for troop movements. Hitler had laid his plans well.

Despite the many assurances of peace in our time, the Government had been making plans should there be a war. Ration books were being printed, air raid sirens were being installed and plans for evacuation of children from large cities were being made. Finally they were preparing for the unthinkable. Unaware of government fears, we believed we were safe on our island home.

I made plans to visit Germany during the summer of 1939. My employers offered me the opportunity to visit the paper factory at Merken-bei-Düren in the Ruhr. I also had contacted Jack Rolfe, the current German teacher at my old school, asking if he could suggest somewhere I could stay in Germany to improve my knowledge of the language.

I thought there still might be a chance of the School Travel Service continuing to operate in the future. Mr. Rolfe suggested that I visit the German professor in Bonn, where he had studied. I had fourteen days holiday. So I planned to spend just a day visiting the factory and the rest of the time with the other foreign students at Doktor Schweiz's home at Schumannstrasse in Bonn. I was looking forward to my trip to another country, especially as Jack Rolfe said he would be visiting Bonn at the same time and would show me round the area.

I set off in late July. Travelling through Belgium to Germany, I was alarmed as we reached the frontier that the train was invaded by fully armed German police. They demanded to inspect our luggage. They opened every suitcase, every bag. They looked at the books and newspapers we were carrying and to my surprise, snatched my copy of Picture Post out of my hands, saying *'Verboten!'* – forbidden. I could not believe it. It seemed an innocuous magazine to me. I wondered what was so dangerous in it that the German people were not allowed to read.

The police's belligerent attitude frightened me. They were very threatening and I could see my fellow travellers, mostly Germans returning from holiday in France, also appeared fearful. As we moved off, the carriage was silent. People were looking at each other suspiciously. I wondered what was in store for me during the next two weeks.

Arriving safely in Essen, I was met by a representative of the paper company. I was driven in an imposing black Mercedes car to the factory at Merken-bei-Düren. We travelled on the autobahn. These first motorways in Germany were wide and straight, lined with trees. I wondered if this was one that Werner had helped to build.

It was an interesting trip and I forgot my fears. The factory was spotless. It was obviously well organised. There were many machines operated by several hundred overalled workers, working industriously and producing all kinds of fancy and decorative papers. They appeared highly disciplined but also ill at ease. They never seemed to smile. This short visit was educational but the atmosphere hardly welcoming. I was glad at the end of the day to return to the car to be escorted back to Essen station and my train journey to Bonn.

On arrival at the Professor's house I found it full of foreign students. They came from many different countries and spoke many languages. They welcomed me and I soon felt at home. I was enjoying a relaxed time with them all. The only slight problem was Sami, an Egyptian boy who had taken a fancy to me. He was a podgy youth whose broken English was almost impossible to understand but he pursued me daily. Finally, when he kept calling up to my window for me to come and join him, in desperation I threw a basin of water over him. That seemed to quench his ardour.

Despite the happy time in the house, there were occasions when I caught glimpses of the sinister side of the Nazi regime. Every shop in the busy centre of Bonn had a framed photo of Hitler in the window. We were highly amused at first when we saw the people giving the Hitler salute to each other as they met. Even when they entered a shop to make their purchases they would click their heels, raise their right arm and say *'Heil Hitler'*, followed by *'Ein kilo Äpfel bitte'*.

On one occasion in a joking mood two of us went into the greengrocers, gave a smart British Army salute and said: 'God save the King and a kilo of plums please,' in our accented German. The shopkeeper did not think it was funny at all; in fact he looked frightened and glanced around him to see if anyone had noticed. I realised then that perhaps our sense of humour was rather different from that of the majority of the German population and we must be careful not to upset anybody. I remembered the police at the border.

Jack Rolfe arrived as promised and I spent a couple of days with him. One morning he took me down to the *Stadtgarten,* the local park, and I sampled a typical German drink of *Apfelwasser,* a type of non-alcoholic cider. It was a pleasant interlude and I was pleased when he told me my German had improved. Two days later several of the students joined me and we went to the park again in the evening. We found a wooden dance floor had been erected. A band was playing and people were dancing. Then the band struck up the familiar tune of the *Lambeth Walk*. So a young Welsh student and I joined the dancers.

The *Lambeth Walk* dance was very popular at the time. It was rather like a London form of a country dance and came from *Me and My Girl*, a revue then showing in London. We started dancing. We had made it round the floor just once when two armed Storm Troopers rushed over, grabbed us and forced us off the floor, throwing us roughly on to the grass. *'Swing ist verboten,'* they shouted. It certainly wasn't Swing but we didn't feel like arguing with them. We picked ourselves up and left hurriedly. That night I wondered what was in store for Germany, for us, for the future. Three days later it was time to return home. It was now early August.

Meanwhile Germany had invaded Poland. The governments of France and Britain issued an ultimatum. Hitler must withdraw his troops from that country or there would be war. The German troops continued their advance. Three weeks after my return, on the morning of September 3rd our government finally declared war on Germany.

On the morning of that memorable day the last letter that I would ever receive from Werner Eisner arrived. He told me he had been drafted into the infantry. I was surprised. Why was a fully trained dentist being used as a foot soldier? It would not be until the end of the war, when his mother wrote to us, asking if we were safe, that I learned the reason. Werner's great grandparents on his father's side were Jewish, the connection not close enough for him to wear the yellow star but instead to be classified as a *second class citizen* and to be used as cannon fodder, as his mother put it ,when she told us he had been killed at Arras in the early months of the war. Soon after, his sister Gea visited me and said that under the same classification, she was sent to Auschwitz, not as a prisoner but as a clerk. Her duties were to list meticulously all the possessions of the Jewish prisoners as they arrived at the death camp. She explained she had never married since the only men she met in those years were the SS guards or the Gestapo.

In the same post as Werner's final letter was a letter from George telling me he had been called up to join his Territorial Unit.

Britain at War

Sunday September 3rd 1939 – a date indelibly marked on the memory of so many of my generation. I remember clearly the scene in our home when we learnt we were at war with Germany. Earlier it had been announced that the Prime Minister, Neville Chamberlain, would be speaking to the nation at 11.15 am. Like many other families, the four of us were gathered in the kitchen.

My parents looked worried. My brother and I were anxious too, we were thinking more about how it would change our lives; a selfish thought but understandable. My father was in his working clothes having just repaired a broken cupboard door; my mother had joined us after preparing the vegetables and a small joint of lamb for our usual Sunday lunch. Dennis and I sat on the edge of our chairs. We were both wearing our best clothes as we had been to Sunday School. I was now a Sunday School teacher. We waited anxiously to hear what the Prime Minister had to say.

For the last few weeks the wireless set – the word radio had not yet entered our vocabulary – was on from the moment we got up until we went to bed. All we seemed to do was listen to the news; what was happening in Europe and the inflammatory speeches of Hitler. We heard how Hitler had invaded Poland and how he had been warned by both Britain and France to remove his troops. The thought of war was on everybody's mind. Of course events prior to that day had made us think it was possible but in our hearts we found it difficult to believe it could happen.

I was just eighteen years of age and my brother only fourteen. We had no idea of the horrors of war but my parents knew only too well. My father had served as a despatch rider in the Great War at the Battle of the Somme and at Passchendaele, first with the Royal Fusiliers and then with the Royal Flying Corps. He had seen death at close quarters and lost many of his comrades, but he would seldom talk about it. My mother was in London during the whole of that terrible war and had lost many of her friends and family. Sometimes she would tell us of the depredation, the lack of food, the fear of being bombed, first by the Zeppelins and later by aeroplanes.

As we waited for the Prime Minister, the memory came back to me of the look of fear on the faces of the Jewish refugees I had travelled with on the train as they left Paris for hoped-for freedom in Britain that previous August of 1938.

The broadcast began. Chamberlain's voice was firm and serious. He sounded sad. We listened intently.

'I am speaking to you from the cabinet room at 10 Downing Street. This morning the British Ambassador in Berlin handed the German government a final note stating that unless we heard from them by 11 o'clock that they were prepared at once to withdraw their troops from Poland, a state of war would exist between us. I have to tell you now that no such undertaking has been received, and that consequently this country is at war with Germany.'

He finished his solemn announcement with the words:

'May God bless you all. And may He defend the right, for it is evil things that we shall be fighting against – brute force, bad faith, injustice,

oppression and persecution, and against them I am certain that right will prevail.'

We sat silently for several minutes – each consumed with our own thoughts. Then my father said: 'We had to do this. We couldn't let Hitler get away with it. We're in for a hard time.' He shook his head.

My mother looked worried. She started laying the table for lunch. 'We still must eat,' she said. 'Dennis, go and finish your homework. Eileen, you can peel the potatoes.'

My brother and I stood up and quietly left the room. I don't know what he was thinking, but my mind was full of so many thoughts. I knew many of my school friends would be sent to fight and perhaps die. Will we be bombed? Will we all die? What can I do to help?

These thoughts suddenly went out of my mind when we were startled by the most terrible wailing sound that seemed to go on and on forever. Would it never stop? We were hearing the first air raid siren of the war – the first of many to come.

'It's an air raid and we haven't put the shelter up yet!' I shouted, and went to rush into the garden where all the heavy pieces of metal lay since the day they were delivered, waiting to be assembled as an Anderson shelter.

My father calmed us all down. 'That wouldn't be any good. It would take far too long. We have to dig a trench first before we can put it up. Far better we wait and see if there is a sound of aircraft and then we can take cover under the stairs.'

He was right. It would take three days to erect that shelter. We listened intently but we could hear nothing, no aircraft seemed to be in our vicinity. After about five minutes we heard the "All Clear" signal, that reassuring single tone of the siren. At that time no-one knew the cause of the warning. It was not mentioned on the wireless, perhaps for security reasons.

It was two years later when I had joined the Women's Auxiliary Air Force that I learnt the cause of that initial alarm. There was no enemy aircraft, no risk of bombing. An RAF operator, using the Watson Watt radio-location system on the North coast of the Thames estuary at Canewdon had made an error in his calculations causing the whole of the south of England to be alerted. He had forgotten to check whether the radio response came from behind or in front of the station.

Up to that morning when we heard Neville Chamberlain announce the declaration of war against Germany we had all been so sure that the politicians would sort something out, the threat would go away. We had tried to ignore the preparations that were already being made.

From September of the previous year, after the Munich meeting, gas marks had been distributed. It is ironic that the first item issued to save the lives of the population would never be needed. I put mine on only once, to test it for size, yet I carried one for the next six years wherever I went.

By April 1939 the public began receiving the parts for building air raid shelters. People living in the centre of London and near the large manufacturing centres were the first recipients. Most families put them in a corner and waited. Then the ration books arrived. Meat, cheese, eggs and butter were to be limited. Coupons would be cut out of the books by the butcher or grocer as we received our weekly or monthly rations. We were advised that many goods would become scarce.

We were notified clothing coupons would be next. All clothing and bedding now manufactured was known as *utility* and bore the iconic sign of two circles with a section cut out, called cheeses or pie crusts. We were encouraged to make do and mend, nothing was thrown away. We unpicked old jumpers and reused the wool. We saved brown paper and string. We grew vegetables instead of flowers.

Pamphlets were delivered advising on necessary air raid precautions. We were warned that the local Air Raid Warden would be on patrol and there would be severe penalties if any lights were showing. Those of us who had electricity replaced the bulbs with lower wattage but many homes were still lit by gas mantles.

From that September day onwards everything changed. Every window in every house was shielded with blackout material. Glass windows and doors were criss-crossed with broad sticky tape to prevent them shattering. Before long, every house or flat in London and most of the rest of the country had been issued with either the Anderson shelter for erection in the garden or the Morrison shelter to be built in an appropriate place inside the house. We were all ready for the expected bombing raids by Hitler's much-vaunted Luftwaffe. We carried our identity card and ration books with us always.

Queues formed at the shops as supplies diminished. Many items disappeared from the shelves. We made friends with our shopkeepers, hoping to persuade them to let us have some little extra that they might have hidden under the counter. It was essential our merchant fleet should not be put in danger by importing unnecessary luxury foods and that only the bare necessities should be carried. Already many of the merchant vessels bringing these goods were being attacked and sunk by Hitler's U-boats. Yet despite the shortages and the many difficulties, I never heard people complain – the British bulldog spirit was showing itself, at least as far as London was concerned.

Daily I would travel by train to the City. The carriages were not so silent now. People were speaking to one another these days, wondering when the bombing would start and comparing notes on what food they had managed to find in the shops; how a supply of lemons had arrived in Southgate, a little more meat was available this week in Camden Town.

In the office of Corke Sons and Company the young men were called up. We would hear from them for a while, telling us where they were and about their training, and then contact faded away. Were they in the British Expeditionary Force, had they gone to France?

The women did jobs they were never allowed to do before, whilst the older men took on heavier workloads. No-one complained. We learnt our bomber force had bombed German cities – but only with pamphlets encouraging the German people to persuade their leader to seek peace. It was a vain hope.

From those early days of September, the children were being evacuated from the large cities. The railway stations would be filled with children, each bearing a label on their clothes giving their name and home address. They carried cardboard boxes with their gas masks.

Children who had never seen a cow found themselves living on farms, families were split up. Cockney accents were heard in Devon market towns. At first they thought it was great fun to be going to the country, just like being on holiday, but many of the town children had difficulty adapting to rural life. The homes where the evacuees were placed found it hard to cope with some of their eating habits. Some children had never seen a proper bath before. As the months went by and the expected bombing of the cities never happened, many of these children were brought home again. It was not what we had anticipated.

From the first day of war we Londoners were expecting immediate air raids. Every night we went to bed prepared to move to the air raid shelter if the siren sounded. Every day we went to work wondering when and where the first bomb would fall. The weeks passed and still nothing happened.

I received the occasional letter from my French pen friend in Lille telling me they dreaded the arrival of the German troops, who were already massed on the border. No German bombers appeared over London. Cinemas shut for a few weeks on the outbreak of war but they soon re-opened. We were lulled into a sense of complacency and life almost seemed to return to normal. We hoped Hitler would stop at the French coast. Many people thought the war would soon be over. We called it *The Phoney War.*

The Phoney War Ends

It was a strange feeling being at war, threatened with air attacks, anticipating the worst – and nothing happening. Everyone was on edge during those first weeks, constantly looking at the sky when an aircraft was heard and then seeing it pass over. 'Must be one of ours,' someone would say.

The wireless was our lifeline. As we travelled each morning to work, the previous night's news was the sole topic of conversation, 'Have you heard that some of the Canadian boys are over here now?' 'They say the RAF is dropping leaflets over Germany.'

The voice of Alvar Liddell on the BBC, calm and controlled, was heard nightly by us all. Many European countries declared their neutrality – Denmark, Sweden, Norway, Holland and Belgium. Now Poland had been taken over completely by the German Wehrmacht. Many people had been killed in the fighting there. Still Britain seemed untouched.

The *Radio Doctor*, Charles Hill, would give us health advice daily. Children were issued with concentrated orange juice and cod-liver oil. The *Food Adviser* told us each morning how to make our rations go farther. I remember the recipe for a nourishing soup – *Keep all your vegetable trimmings and any meat bones, boil them all together in water and add any pieces of stale bread. This will thicken the soup. A little salt and pepper will improve the flavour.* We called it Hitler's Revenge!

Czechoslovakia would be the next target for Hitler's troops. Again the Jews were being rounded up. Reports were sketchy but I remembered the words in the letters from Hali Nelb, how her beloved Fuhrer was going to get rid of all the Jews and I feared the worst for them. I remembered Kristallnacht in November 1938 when the first mass killing and imprisonment of the Jews in Germany took place.

Our lives continued comparatively normally except for rationing, the blackout and shortages. On January 8th 1940 bacon, butter and sugar were rationed; eight ounces of bacon or ham, sixteen ounces of sugar and eight ounces of butter per person per week. This was followed by meat, tea, jam, cheese, eggs, milk, biscuits and breakfast cereals. For those with cars, petrol was rationed. Imported goods became scarcer. We had not seen a banana or orange for weeks. We were warned that clothing coupons would be issued. We were encouraged to *make do and mend*. Our merchant shipping was being harried night and day by the U-boats and reports of sinkings were frequent. But we were still safe.

By now the shop-fitting firm Harold Lebus, where my father worked, had been taken over completely for war work and he was doing extra hours. My mother took over more duties in the office of my father's firm as the young men had all gone. My brother, now fifteen, was working for his General Schools Certificate and Matriculation but many of his teachers had been called up and classes became larger. Retired women teachers returned to fill the gaps in the timetable and many extra-curricular school activities ceased. There were fewer sporting facilities, air raid shelters had been built on the playing fields.

The cinema was one of the few entertainments in the early days of war still open and the Movietone News brought us pictures of German troops on the march. Most of the theatres shut down as actors and backstage personnel were called up. Only the Windmill Theatre stayed open every night throughout the war.

Christmas came and went; a more frugal one than usual and with little celebration. People in the street looked anxious. In the shops or the train, people were asking: 'When will Hitler attack us?' 'Do you think our troops will beat the Jerries?' 'Have you heard from your son lately?' 'Has your brother been called up yet?' Everyone had someone "over there" in France. We entered a new year, 1940.

Travelling at night was difficult. All street lamps were dimmed. There were no lights in the shop windows and vehicles had their headlights reduced to slits. Yet somehow, despite all the gloom, the British sense of humour kept us going and although people complained of food shortages I never remember anybody talking about defeat.

In April I was surprised to receive a letter from the Scottish Provident Institution, the company I had joined on leaving school and where I worked before I went to France.

'Dear Miss Le Croissette, We would like to offer you a post back with our company.' Many of their male employees had volunteered for the Services or had been called up and, as I had been trained, they wanted me to fill their place. They offered me a much larger salary. I found the offer tempting, especially as they had evacuated their City office to Surrey.

My current work with the paper agents offered little challenge as they had lost all their overseas supplies of speciality papers. I thought about having to leave my family in London but, as there was no sign of any enemy bombing, I decided to accept the offer and move to Woking.

It was strange living and working in a large house surrounded by beautiful grounds on the outskirts of a pleasant town, instead of in a City office in the middle of the business centre of London. It was a great relief not having to face the daily train journeys and sandwich lunches on the seat outside the Royal Exchange.

On arrival I was allocated an enormous bedroom overlooking the garden, with a vast mahogany wardrobe. My pathetic collection of clothes was lost in it. I was to sleep in a double bed for the first time. This time I was a valued employee – no more scratchy maroon overalls. Now women were needed. I did find it lonely at first as I was much younger than the rest of the staff, which consisted of – to me – boring men too old to be called up and a few senior women. So I looked for something to do in the evenings that would be useful.

At first on most weekends, I would return home to my family. The journey back to London by train was an ordeal. The carriages were crowded with troops and usually all the seats were taken, so it meant standing in the corridor for the whole journey. There would be little room to move and a trip to the toilet would be like an obstacle race over kitbags and rifles, suitcases and tin hats. The accents around me would vary from broad Cornish to indecipherable Geordie, with an occasional Canadian or Australian voice amongst them. But there was always someone to help me off the train and rescue my luggage from the surrounding pile.

Woking was the nearest centre for any entertainment for soldiers training in the nearby Inkerman Barracks. Most of the young soldiers were from Scottish regiments, the Kings Own Scottish Borderers or the Black Watch, as well as men from the Royal Army Service Corps. I especially recall the Kosbies in their smart tartan trews and their cockaded caps.

Looking for somewhere to spend my leisure hours, I found the YMCA was running a canteen in the centre of the town and asking for helpers. I thought this might be a way of doing something useful, so I volunteered. And there I had my first taste of catering, albeit at a fairly low level, little realising that in the years to come I would go on to be an hotelier.

From behind the canteen counter, serving out large mugs of tea and home-made cakes, I met many of these young Scotsmen. Most had never left their homeland before, they were young and vulnerable and very lonely. Their accents varied from the delightful burr of the Lowlands to the special brogue of the Highlands. They were only too happy to have female company. I went out dancing with several of them at their barracks, perhaps once or twice. One day they were there and then we never saw them again – sent off to France to the British Expeditionary Force. I often wonder how many survived.

It was the early spring of 1940 when everything changed. On April 9th Germany invaded Denmark on the pretext of preserving their neutrality. The Danes put up little resistance against this vast army. Norway was the next target, as Hitler needed to safeguard access to the northern port of Narvik. This small country did offer some resistance but the Norwegian leader, a Fascist supporter, gave in almost at once. He created a National Socialist Government. His name was Quisling, a word that from then on became synonymous with traitor. We later learnt that British and French troops had landed in Northern Norway and occupied the Faroe Islands but after a heavy German assault they had to withdraw. Soon Germany had overrun the whole country.

We would listen to the news reports and wonder if Hitler would ever stop his advance. At the cinema Movietone News would show reports from neutral American journalists and we would ask ourselves how it was all going to end.

On May 10th German troops crossed into Holland. A few hours later, Winston Churchill took over as Prime Minister from Neville Chamberlain, who had resigned as both the Labour and Liberal parties refused to work with him after the failed Allied incursion into Norway. Churchill later wrote that at that moment, 'I felt that I was walking with destiny.'

By June, Hitler's Wehrmacht had moved through Holland and Belgium and entered France through Alsace. We had heard so much about the strength of the Maginot Line, we thought the Nazi onslaught would be held there by a strong French defence, backed up by our troops. But the Germans by-passed it with ease. In the then quiet and untouched Britain, we began to worry for friends and family serving at the front with the Expeditionary Force.

My boyfriend George was already in France. I had received very occasional letters from him but had heard nothing for a month. These letters when they came were short and gave no idea where he was or what he was doing. He wrote each time: 'I am thinking of you and hoping you are safe.' And he would add: 'Write soon.' Nothing more. I had no idea whether he was near the fighting. Any reply I sent went to the British Forces Post Office wherever that was.

I tried to remain optimistic but it was hard not to worry. I thought of the other boys who had been at school with me, some of whom had already died. Doug Ferguson, whose zest for life was immeasurable and who had been a keen Boy Scout, had been killed. The irrepressible Bobby Johnson was lost at sea. It was hard to imagine that someone so full of life had died so young. It seemed unreal. Those boys I had cheered on the football pitch only a short while before were *over there*, fighting to save France and dying there. The nightly news reported that the Wehrmacht was forcing its way through with apparent ease, supported by waves of aircraft.

Gradually we realised that our forces were retreating towards the coast. It could have been annihilation if the German High Command had not decided to halt and refit their army prior to attacking the French defences further south. It was only this that gave the British Expeditionary Force time to reach the coast and plan a retreat by sea – a defeat that we have since revered as a victory.

The Glory of the Defeat

The news was grim. From late May we knew our soldiers were in retreat. We heard how the Germans had come through the Ardennes at the same time as invading Holland and Belgium. Backed up by their strong air power, they were rapidly forcing the BEF back towards the coast. I tried to stop thinking that George may have already been taken prisoner or even been killed.

It was hard to concentrate on work. Everyone in the office had someone close to them in the Expeditionary Force and we had the wireless on all our waking hours – listening, hoping for good news. By late spring, many of our troops had managed to reach the coast around Dunkirk and Operation Dynamo was being launched to rescue them.

It was then that the people of Britain came to the rescue. Every *little ship* possible sailed towards Dunkirk. Fishing vessels, private launches, pleasure steamers headed for the French coast to join the ships of the Navy. They were crewed by old sailors, fishermen, leisure yachtsmen, women, anyone who could help. These smaller craft were able to get the men off the beaches and ferry them to the larger vessels offshore.

It was two weeks I shall never forget; waiting for news, hearing rumours, not knowing the truth. As the days passed, more and more troops were pulled off the beaches despite heavy aerial bombardment. There were many fatalities and even more men injured but finally more than 330,000 reached our shores.

Because of the vast numbers arriving, the survivors were put on trains and moved away from the coastal ports as soon as they arrived. Woking station was the first stop for many of those rescued and the YMCA had set up feeding stations on the platforms.

All the volunteers were asked to assist for as many hours as possible and my office manager willingly gave permission for me to work full-time there. Trestle tables were erected and teams of people made hundreds of sandwiches, whilst others baked cakes at home from their precious rations and brought them in throughout those historic days. There were vast pots of soup kept hot on primus stoves. The tea urns were always full.

As each train arrived, the soldiers poured on to the platform and descended on the food. Some had not eaten for several days and had only what remained in their water bottles to drink. Many were soaked to the skin having swum out to the boats, their uniforms torn and bloodied. All were hungry and tired, their faces etched with anguish and strain. Yet given a mug of hot tea and some food, they smiled and thanked us and then in a few short minutes were ordered back to the train and on to their next destination. In no time another train would arrive and more hungry and tired men would be looking for something to eat and a friendly greeting. The badly injured were taken to hospital as soon as they landed but those with minor injuries were just patched up and put on the trains.

Scattered amongst the British were the few French and occasional Polish or Czech soldiers and airmen who had managed to join the Allies on their way to the coast and to rescue. On the third day a train arrived and from a carriage almost opposite to where I was serving a young French airman alighted. I did not notice him at first but he came over to me for a mug of tea. Then his face lit up and he cried out: '*Mon Dieu, Eileen mon amie!*' and he hugged me and kissed me. He was crying.

You can imagine my surprise and then joy to find it was René Cadier. A crazy coincidence at a crazy time! I had met him about three years earlier at the house of my music teacher, a widow, Mrs. Elias. She would take in foreign students during the holidays to earn a little extra money. Her music students used to mix with these visitors and René and I had become friends during his stay and then exchanged the odd letter in the following year.

Now once more he had come into my life in such a strange way. We had little time to talk but he said he had flown his aircraft until it had run out of fuel. He had landed in a field, destroyed the plane and joined the soldiers on a nearby road, making his way on foot to Dunkirk. Hardly having enough time to drink his tea, he was ordered to rejoin the train. He managed to tell me his family lived in Pau in the Pyrenees and then he was gone – but not before I pushed a packet of sandwiches into his hand. He waved from the window as the train pulled out.

I never thought we would ever meet again but years later, driving over the Pyrenees with my husband, we called in to Pau and I decided to try and find him. Looking in the local telephone directory, there was his name. I took the chance of calling at the address and we met once more. He was by now a Senior Pilot in Air France, married and with a young family. He was a survivor.

Rescued troops kept arriving until the first week in June, every day more trains and more shattered remnants of the British Expeditionary Force. We continued to serve them and be cheered as more and more were rescued from those beaches of northern

France. It was a miracle so many of our troops managed to return home against such great odds. We knew that although many were left behind, lying dead on the beaches or imprisoned in the hands of the Nazis, thanks to the skill and determination of the Royal Navy and the *little ships*, victory had been salvaged from an inglorious defeat.

The fleet of ships involved in the action amounted to over a thousand. In the darkest hour, at the beginning of Operation Dynamo, it was thought perhaps 35,000 troops might return home before the enemy troops captured Dunkirk. Because of the decision by the Germans to stop their advance to the west and first capture the northern part of France, over 350,000 Allied troops reached our shores. The Dunkirk Spirit was born.

It was to be over a month before I learnt that George was safely home, only to be sent off to another front without my seeing him. All he managed was a quick phone call from the railway station. It was not until 2006 that I learnt how he had escaped from Dunkirk.

Together with another sergeant in the Military Police, he was detailed to act as beachmaster, organising the ferrying of the soldiers to the vessels offshore. He could see a cargo vessel half a mile out to sea, so he searched for a means to get his men out to it. During the final days he came across a large rowing boat complete with oars. Having been a keen member of Staines Rowing Club, with a fellow Military Policeman he had rowed ten times out to this Dutch freighter, each journey carrying eight soldiers. George and his fellow oarsman were by then completely exhausted. Finally the skipper said: 'That's enough, no more. Jump aboard you two!'

Dangerous Days

After Dunkirk, more stragglers managed to make their way to Cherbourg evading capture and they too were rescued. But German troops were moving rapidly through France. Paris had been entered and by June 22nd, France had surrendered. The following day, Hitler made a triumphant victory parade through Paris passing under the iconic Arc de Triomphe with his troops.

My heart bled for France and I thought of the people I knew there. I wondered about my friend, Yvette Reynaud in Lille. Had she and her family survived? I wondered too about the Boucher family and those three children I taught English to, over two years ago. I knew their mother owned an hotel in Paris. I wondered whether that family, for the sake of their business interests, would fraternise with the invaders. Were the French now giving the *Heil Hitler* salute as they did their shopping?

I had by now resumed my duties at the office but every Friday I would travel home to North London, returning on an early train on Monday morning. Conversation was all about where Hitler would strike next. Few of my friends were left in London. Those who had not volunteered for one or other of the Forces, or had been conscripted, were either evacuated with the companies they worked for or doing volunteer work with the Home Guard or the Fire Service. Germany had now occupied all northern France, leaving the south to be ruled by the so-called neutral Vichy government. We feared things here would soon change. The atmosphere was tense. We were alone now.

Lord Haw-Haw, as he was nicknamed – was William Joyce, a renegade born in America but brought up in Ireland – and one of Mosley's key Blackshirts who fled to Berlin in 1939. He delivered daily propaganda broadcasts boasting of German successes. Now he threatened that the invasion of our island was imminent. We were not to know that already Hitler was planning *Operation Sealion*, the codename adopted for the invasion of Britain. A fleet of barges was being prepared off the French coast.

However, our Government was already making preparations. Road signs were being removed and vital buildings were sandbagged. One of my cousins, living on the south coast, wrote: 'We are very worried. All the beaches here are being mined and barbed wire defences are being erected all around us.'

The Home Guard had been formed as the first line of defence. It consisted of older men, over the call-up age, often armed only with spades and broomsticks. My brother and two of his friends, then aged fifteen, had volunteered to act as messengers during air raids, using their bicycles to transport urgent information between the Home Guard and the Fire Station.

My father was working long hours overtime on Ministry of Defence orders. New armaments were being designed. Aero engineers had designed an aircraft made from wood. He never told us they were making it at his factory. It was only very much later that he said: 'Did you know I designed the tail fin of the Mosquito?' My mother, working in the office of the same company, was ordering the materials for troop-carrying gliders – the Horsa was produced in the thousands and would play an important part in the Normandy landings.

It was at this time that large notices appeared on the billboards – *DIG FOR VICTORY*, encouraging us to grow vegetables in our suburban gardens; *BE LIKE DAD, KEEP MUM*, a witty warning not to talk about war work in the factories or discuss details of troop movements, and *WOMEN OF BRITAIN, COME INTO THE FACTORIES*, asking wives at home to do their bit for their country.

Rumours went around that spies were being dropped by parachute in Scotland and Wales. We were warned there could be traitors in our midst and that careless talk cost lives. The whole country was being reminded to do all in its power to preserve our nation.

Those too old to work in the arms factories or to join the Forces did their bit. They learnt how to use stirrup pumps to put out fires, the women ran canteens for the troops or knitted socks and balaclava helmets for the colder nights. By now the Women's Land Army had been formed to free agricultural workers to join the forces. They would ensure that our food production would be maintained. Young men, amongst them conscientious objectors, were sent down the mines to ensure coal supplies did not run out. They were called Bevin Boys after the Labour Party politician, Ernest Bevin. The whole country realised there were perilous days ahead and we must all pull together; rich and poor, old and young.

Meanwhile the Royal Navy was having many successes. Hitler realised that as our Navy was superior to his smaller naval force, it was essential to break the morale of the RAF and reduce its fighting power if he were to have any chance of a successful invasion of Britain.

By the summer of 1940 there were officially over 9,000 trained pilots in the Royal Air Force for around 5,000 aircraft, mostly bombers. Aircraft production was adding more than 300 planes a week and soon outstripping the number of operational pilots free to fly them. However, many pilots were engaged in training other pilots either in Britain or in Canada, whilst too many were in staff positions and not flying.

This caused grave concern to Air Chief Marshal Hugh "Stuffy" Dowding, in charge of Fighter Command. On July 1st 1940 he could only draw on just over a thousand fighter pilots from the regular RAF, Auxiliary Air Force and Volunteer Reserve. Intelligence had told him that Germany had many more aircrew available and a large number of these were already experienced in aerial combat due to their actions in Spain in support of General Franco during the recent Civil War.

Those of us, just carrying on life as best we could, had no idea what was going on behind the scenes. News was restricted and we only heard what was considered necessary. All mail from the troops was censored and sometimes letters would arrive with much of the writing blacked out. I had not seen George since his return from Dunkirk. His last letter said: 'I am at a training camp prior to being sent overseas.' But he could not say where or when.

It was now almost a year since we had last been together and so much had happened to him. I wondered how much he had changed and whether he still loved me. I tried to make my letters to him interesting but there was little to say. The newspapers reported that Hitler's ally, Italy, was fighting in North Africa and had recently invaded British Somaliland, so I wondered if that was where he would be sent. I just hoped I would be able to see him before he was sent overseas again.

The British public did not know that from 1935 an early form of radio direction finding was being developed. Robert Watson Watt, a Scottish physicist and a descendant of James Watt of steam engine renown, was initially approached to investigate the possibility of building a death ray using radio waves. He told the Air Ministry he considered this impractical but suggested a method might be devised to give advance warning of an air attack. Sonic responses had been received by naval vessels from icebergs and Watson Watt wondered whether radio waves could act similarly and give a response from aircraft. He suggested that a network of radio echo detection units should be built with a possible range of 200 miles, capable of giving such an advance warning.

He proved his point when a demonstration showed that a receiver was able to pick up echoes of a transmission by the BBC Daventry tower from an approaching aircraft target. The demonstration so impressed the authorities, especially Air Marshal Sir Hugh Dowding that a sum of £10,000 was awarded to pursue the development of a warning system. Watson Watt set up a research station first at Orfordness and later at Bawdsey Manor on the east coast. This was to lead to radiolocation – first called RDF, range and direction finding, and then Radar.

Both the USA and Germany had investigated similar usage of radio waves but it was the brilliant conception of Watson Watt to use it as a national network, which became known as the CH (Chain Home) system, giving Britain a defence weapon that would prove invaluable. People living on the south coast would wonder at the series of metal towers, some over 300 feet high, which were being erected near our seaside towns. They were unaware that this chain of Radar stations would ensure our small fleet of fighter planes were used in the most efficient way when the German offensive began, despite our desperate shortage of aircraft and trained pilots.

Hitler's air offensive began on August 12th. German Intelligence was now aware that Britain had an early warning system in operation and they assumed the towers on the coast were part of it. An attack on these installations was the first priority. That day Nazi bombers targeted Britain for the first time. We were only told that several coastal units had been hit. But that evening things changed for all of us. We realised that Britain was destined to be Hitler's next and perhaps final victim.

The initial raids caused little damage to the Radar stations and they were repaired very rapidly. Within six hours, most of the stations hit were on the air again. The towers themselves were a difficult target. Fortunately the enemy omitted to destroy the supporting installations such as telephone relays and power stations, which would have had a far greater effect.

Very soon Goering, the head of the German Air Force, decided to change tactics. The initial attacks were followed by heavy raids on the coastal airfields. The German fighter force then proceeded to attack inland fighter stations. We lost many planes during this time both on the ground and in the air, despite the pilots attempting to take off as soon as a warning was received. Our already small fighter force was being depleted.

Londoners would hear the throbbing of the German planes and could recognise their sound. It was different from that of our own fighters, deeper and somehow more ominous. We would look up in the sky and see them overhead, every time wondering when the civilian population would be the next target.

Whether living in London or in surrounding areas, we could see the dogfights above us in the blue summer skies and frequently witnessed one or other of the planes falling to the ground. The sound of gunfire from the ack-ack units sited in our parks and open spaces pounded our ears both day and night.

August 15th saw the heaviest attack on our airfields and the 18th was the day when most casualties on both sides were reported. The sometimes-exaggerated numbers of kills by our pilots reported on the BBC, and the vastly inflated losses of our aircraft announced by Lord Haw-Haw, made it difficult to understand how successful the enemy attacks were. But it was obvious both sides were sustaining heavy losses of both men and machines.

The Luftwaffe was also losing trained crews as well as aircraft, whereas our fighter pilots often managed to bale out on home territory and lived to fight another day. In late August, the newly promoted Generalfeldmarshall Goering, changed tack yet again, ordering attacks on the aircraft factories in addition to the RAF's airfields. Plymouth and Birmingham were bombed and the first civilian casualties reported.

On the night of the 24th the first bombs fell on London. The evening news broadcast told us the East End was ablaze. I telephoned my mother the following day and she said: 'It was frightening. We could hear the bombs and see the flames from here.' I felt terrible, leaving my family to face the threat alone whilst I was in comparative safety outside the London area.

Returning home that weekend, the first damage to the capital could be seen from the train – houses with whole sides missing, bedrooms open to public view, belongings strewn on the pavements, and people walking the streets with dazed looks on their faces. History has told us that the first bombing of the civil population was unintended at that time and caused by pilot error. Only the docks were supposed to be the target.

The bombing of London had a powerful and enraging effect on Churchill. Until now we had never targeted enemy civilian areas. He ordered that Berlin should be bombed in retaliation. The first of these raids took place on August 25th and outraged Hitler, who had constantly been assured by Goering that the German people and their cities would be safe. He ordered the bombing of British cities without mercy. 'Our great Fuhrer has vowed to obliterate the cities of Britain,' Lord Haw-Haw told us in his nightly broadcast. That was when the real terror started; the London Blitz began. I realised it was time I did something more useful, but what?

The Blitz

Donner und Blitzen – German for thunder and lightning – and the source of the emotive description of the terrible retaliatory air offensive by Hitler after Berlin was bombed. The daily and nightly bombing of London is known to this day as The Blitz.

It started on a weekend as I was returning home from my duties in Woking. The train was arriving at Paddington station in the late afternoon of September 7th, 1940 when I became aware of a cacophony of sounds. As we arrived at the platform we could hear the ack-ack guns in action. They were sited in the public parks and on spare ground in the city. The silver of the balloon barrage, now dotted around London, shone in the light of the gunfire. These balloons, tethered on steel cables from lorries, acted as a deterrent to low flying bombers and had the effect of making bomb-aiming less accurate.

The sky was lit up – as the BBC later described it *'by the glare and the flare of the star shells.'* The scene was enhanced by the criss-crossing beams of searchlights. The dull throb of aircraft engines filled the air, punctuated by the sounds of guns firing. As we left the train and moved from the station we looked up to the sky. We could see the shadowy silhouettes of the enemy planes above us. We could hear too the dull thump of bombs as they landed. Our London was being attacked. Already smoke and flames could be seen coming from the area around the Docks. This was to be the Luftwaffe's initial target and our baptism of fire.

THE BLITZ

As I made my way down into the Piccadilly Underground station I wondered how many civilians would be killed that night. As the train passed through the stations towards Wood Green it was obvious many people were using the platforms as air raid shelters. They were full of people just sitting or standing, clutching belongings, many with children. They looked bewildered. They made no attempt to board the train – they stood there transfixed.

Arriving home at Winchmore Hill I could see from our upstairs windows an orange-red haze in the sky in the direction of the River Thames. Was this the beginning of hell for the people of London? The raid seemed to go on for hours, it was impossible to sleep.

Next morning, it was reported that over 300 bombers had attacked London in waves, escorted by an even larger number of fighter aircraft. We had not been able to put up much resistance and no bombers were reported to have been shot down. Much of the bombing had been inaccurate, missing the target. Instead they had landed on the streets and houses nearby. On this first night of the Blitz 450 Londoners were killed and very many more were injured.

We were not to know that at that time few of our fighter aircraft were able to operate successfully at night. Searchlights had only a limited height at which they were effective and there were initially not enough ack-ack guns in place in and around the capital. Londoners felt terrifyingly vulnerable. Everyone wondered if the raid would be repeated. We soon learnt the answer to that.

The following night and for a further 55 days and nights the bombing would continue. The death toll of civilians, especially in the East End, was mounting nightly. It seemed that even the weather was kind to the enemy. Not until November was there a break when fog grounded the German air force. But it was only a very short respite and London's suffering would go on until May 1941.

As I returned to Woking on the Sunday after the first weekend of bombing I could see from the train the vast areas of destruction. The terrible damage to houses and shops was clearly visible. Through the gaping holes in the sides of houses could be seen the shattered remains of people's homes. From the conversation in the carriage, already some people had lost family or friends in these first days of bombing.

Several passengers living in these areas that had been so badly damaged described to us the horrors they had witnessed. I worried about leaving my parents and my brother still in London. I tried to take comfort from the fact that they lived in a northern suburb away from the docks and manufacturing area, and so far it seemed those were the areas at risk.

Already the evacuated children who had returned home at the time of the phoney war were being sent back. Yet it became obvious that Londoners, although frightened, were more angry and indignant that their city was being targeted. Their resolve, to resist in any way they could, hardened. They became resilient. They learnt to cope. The platforms of the Tube stations became home when theirs were destroyed. Along the length of the platforms metal bunk beds were put up by the local authorities. Families would camp there, cooking makeshift meals over small paraffin stoves. Their only washing facilities were the hand basins in the toilets, which were soon overwhelmed with use.

As the days passed, signs of strain appeared on the faces of these people living in the Tube. The faces of little children who were living underground for so long took on a yellowed hue. Yet as the train arrived, often I would hear these refugees from the Blitz singing together – '*Run Rabbit, Run Rabbit, Run Run Run,*' followed by Vera Lynn's emotive ballad '*There'll always be an England, And England will be free, If England means as much to you, As England means to me.*' They were determined to make the best of a bad situation.

On October 15th London had its heaviest raid of the war. By now our fighters were succeeding in shooting down many of the bombers. Germany was losing both aircraft and crews. For some time the daytime dropping of incendiaries had preceded the night raids. On this particular night it looked as if the whole of London was on fire. Yet despite these days and nights of terror, Hitler's avowed intention to break the spirit of the British people had the opposite effect.

We became more resolute to join in the fight against a common foe. Rich and poor, young and old, worked together, helping each other, offering their services wherever needed and remaining steadfast. I can remember two aged sisters living in our road would wait for the All Clear and then go out in the street and shake their walking sticks at the sky, shouting: 'You won't beat us, you Nazis.' I never heard a defeatist word throughout all those terrible days.

Of course there were black marketeers making money out of the shortage of goods. They would approach you in the street offering forged clothing coupons or items of food, no doubt stolen, at a high price to supplement our rations. There will always be someone taking advantage of any shortage in war or peace. But most people made the best of the difficulties of day to day living.

My mother would tell me how difficult it was to find something different to feed the family. Already our garden was producing potatoes, Brussels sprouts and peas. The fishmongers were now offering whale meat and snoek. People would try them but found the oily flavour of whale unpleasant. There was very little other fish obtainable. The Government now issued to all concentrated orange juice and cod liver oil tablets to supplement the diet.

There would be grumblings at the butchers when the housewives saw the size of their weekly ration of meat. 'How can we feed our growing kids on that,' they would say. 'Haven't you got some sausages or perhaps a heart you could let me have?' Every bit of offal from a sheep or lamb or bullock was used. Amazingly people would make do; nothing was wasted and nobody starved. The daily bombing went on but gradually our fighters were having greater and greater success.

As the weeks went by other cities were bombed – Plymouth, Southampton, Bristol, Cardiff, Manchester, Liverpool and many more; never so consistently nor as often as London but still causing civilian deaths and great damage to homes, factories, schools and churches. On the night of November 14/15th, Coventry was targeted, destroying vast areas of this industrial city including its Cathedral. That raid has remained in public memory to this day. Londoners learnt they were not alone; other cities were now suffering the same horrors, the same fears.

It was on the night of December 29/30th, that the people of London felt most threatened. That night the dropping of thousands of incendiaries over the City caused a firestorm around

St. Paul's Cathedral and the Guildhall. Winston Churchill, realising the symbolism of St. Pauls, sent out a message: 'Protect it at all costs.' Miraculously, after hours of bombing and destruction around it, St. Paul's remained comparatively unscathed. The London Fire Service had saved the day.

The newspapers called it The Second Fire of London. It was a night Londoners would never forget when the very heart of their city was the target. Ernest Pyle, one of WW2's most popular journalists, described it in the following words:

"The greatest of all the fires was directly in front of us. Flames seemed to whip hundreds of feet into the air. Pinkish-white smoke ballooned upward in a great cloud, and out of this cloud there gradually took shape – so faintly at first that we weren't sure we saw correctly – the gigantic dome of St. Paul's Cathedral. St. Paul's was surrounded by fire, but it came through. It stood there in its enormous proportions – growing slowly clearer and clearer, the way objects take shape at dawn. It was like a picture of some miraculous figure that appears before peace-hungry soldiers on a battlefield.

Later on I borrowed a tin hat and went out among the fires. That was exciting too; but the thing I shall always remember above all the other things in my life is the monstrous loveliness of that one single view of London on a holiday night – London stabbed with great fires, shaken by explosions, its dark regions along the Thames sparkling with the pin points of white-hot bombs, all of it roofed over with a ceiling of pink that held bursting shells, balloons, flares and the grind of vicious engines. And in yourself the excitement and anticipation and wonder in your soul that this could be happening at all."

His words took me back to those days when I worked so close to St. Paul's and often used to visit it during the lunch hour. It was where I could feel the pulsing heartbeat of the great City of

London. His words still remain a permanent record in my mind of those terrible days.

Even though I spent four nights of the week out of London at Woking we would still feel the effects of the raids there. Many of the returning German bombers, either damaged or short of fuel, would offload their bombs as they returned home. No-one was safe. The noise of the guns and the roar of the explosions filled our ears night and day. Shrapnel fell constantly. But as the weeks passed, the news of greater success by our fighter pilots was music to our ears. Increasing numbers of German bombers failed to return home and it was suspected that their factories were not keeping up with necessary replacements for their losses.

Meanwhile our factories were producing increasing numbers of Spitfires and Hurricanes and Fighter Command was training more pilots, many of them coming from our colonies. What we were not told was that British scientists were perfecting Radar installations on land and in aircraft. The chain of Radar stations around our coast relaying their information to the secret Filter Room of Fighter Command, had provided advance warning to the fighter stations, allowing our squadrons to be used most efficiently.

Night fighters were now equipped with a special device ensuring improved success against the enemy bombers. It was announced that this was due to the pilots being fed a special diet supplement of carrots. The newspapers cited the amazing results by the pilot "Cats Eyes" Cunningham in shooting down the enemy at night. This ploy prevented the Germans learning about the boffins' newest top-secret invention called A.I or Air Interception Radar. So successful was the bogus cover story that even today many people still believe that carrots improve your eyesight!

The London Blitz continued until May 10th 1941, culminating with attacks on our seaports. By then our successes in destroying enemy aircraft increased considerably. In January Fighter Command shot down only 28, by May this had risen to 124. Hitler's plan to gain air supremacy had not succeeded. Realising he had failed; he made the fatal decision to open a second front in Russia and postpone *Operation Sealion,* the planned invasion of Britain, indefinitely. We did not then realise the important part played by Radar, especially due to the inspired strategy of its use as a continuous chain of defence around our coast. But by the time the Blitz on London ended, I too would become a small link in that Radar chain.

Decision Time

A rising feeling of patriotism was growing throughout the country in these months of fear and danger during the Blitz. Many of the boys who were at school with me had already volunteered for the Services long before they were due to be conscripted. My favourite cousin Eric Padfield, two years older than I was, had volunteered several months before the war for the Royal Air Force. He had always wanted to fly.

He was sent to RAF Halton for initial technical training where he excelled. At the end of his course he was awarded the Lord Wakefield Scholarship, given only to the best trainee, and this meant he would go on to the college at RAF Cranwell for training as a pilot. Very soon he gained his wings and was commissioned as Pilot Officer Padfield.

He was chosen to become an instructor rather than go on immediate operations. It was essential new pilots were trained swiftly to replace the many losses Fighter Command had sustained. Training lasted only a very short time and the recruits had to learn quickly. Newly trained pilots were being sent to operational fighter stations with perhaps fewer than fifteen hours solo flying under their belt. Many lasted no more than one or two missions.

Eric was flying and instructing for many hours daily. The pressures were great. It was during a heavy summer storm in August 1940 that the accident happened. The aircraft he was in crashed. The weather had been frightful but trainee pilots had to get experience in all conditions. Eric and the three trainees aboard were killed instantly. To this day, I still do not know who piloted the aircraft, my cousin or one of the trainees.

Eric's mother, my father's youngest sister, never got over the tragedy of losing her only son and a few years later took her own life. I was also deeply affected by his death. It made me realise that helping in a YMCA canteen and working in a comparatively safe and comfortable office was not enough. I had to do more for my country.

My father had volunteered during World War One to transfer to the newly formed Royal Flying Corps. His youngest brother was already in the RAF and now Eric was gone. There was no question in my mind as to which service I would apply. I must replace him.

I told my parents of my decision and my father said at once: 'You are old enough to make up your own mind. We will always support you. Follow your heart.' So it was in November of that year I sent in my application to the Air Ministry to join the Women's Auxiliary Air Force. I was just nineteen years of age.

There were many such applications arriving daily at the Air Ministry and I was informed that there would be a delay before my interview. However, by early January 1941 I received a letter telling me to report to Adastral House on February 12th. Two weeks prior to this, I had by chance met up with an old school friend, Mary True. We had both competed in the local district school sports on several occasions and we would run against each other in the 100 yards sprint.

I was surprised to see her looking very smart in a WAAF uniform. 'I didn't know you had joined up,' I said. 'I'm joining the WAAF too. I'm going for my interview in a couple of weeks.' I plied her with questions – what was life like in the Services, what did she do, was she happy? Her reply was enthusiastic.

'It's a great life – a lot of hard work but what I am doing is interesting and very worthwhile.' She would not tell me what she did but she added: 'I will give you some very good advice. When the recruiting officer asks you what branch you want to go in, she is sure to say – Cook or Driver! Tell her neither, just say you want to be a Clerk Special Duties.' I asked her what sort of work that entailed but she refused to tell me any more. 'I am not allowed to say.' Then after a moment she added: 'Just tell them you are good at mathematics.' She had remembered that it was my best subject at school!

Two days later at the recruiting office at the Air Ministry in London this is exactly what happened. I was ushered into the office where a rather large and important-looking WAAF officer was seated behind an enormous oak desk. 'Sit down,' she said. 'What trade do you want to go in, cook or driver?'

I answered immediately: 'Neither, I want to be a Clerk Special Duties.'

She looked aghast and said: 'How did you learn about this trade?'

I explained how I had met a friend who was now a WAAF and asked her advice and she had suggested I apply for the same category she was in. I had to assure the officer that my friend had given nothing away about her work but that she had told me to explain that I was good at maths. As soon as I said that, there was no argument.

'Right, I'll put you down for CSD. Good luck, you'll need to work very hard.' I wondered what I had let myself in for.

Then came all the routine checks, a stringent medical examination followed by an eyesight test. I was sent to another office where a sergeant asked for details of my education and whether I had any special qualifications. That all went well – then there was a snag. Someone in the backroom queried my name.

Eileen Le Croissette sounded foreign, was I a risk? As it was a French name and France was our ally, I couldn't understand why there was a problem. I was asked to produce my birth certificate. Fortunately I had brought all my documents with me. I explained that the name came from my Huguenot Protestant ancestors who had escaped to Britain in 1698 after persecution in France following the Revocation of the Edict of Nantes. So they decided I was British enough to be accepted!

I was told I would receive my call-up papers within a few weeks. They would include a travel warrant and instructions as to where I had to report for initial training. It was emphasised that I should not bring a lot of luggage with me and not to miss the train. I returned home full of excitement and anticipation. I would now write to George and tell him I'd joined up, and notify the office I would be resigning. I hoped my contribution would help my country. I was British and proud of it.

The New Recruit

The next few weeks seemed interminable. I knew my call-up papers would be sent to my parents' address. Each evening I would finish work and immediately phone home. 'Has anything come yet? Isn't there a letter for me?'

Day after day the answer would be: 'No dear, not yet.' I would go back to my room, dejected. I was so anxious to start my new life, every day seemed wasted. Work seemed so unimportant – sending out premium notices for life insurance, when I could be doing something useful to fight Hitler.

Then finally on March 2nd the telephonist called across the office: 'Someone wants you on the phone.' My mother had contacted the office as soon as the post had arrived that morning.

'It's come?' I asked.

'Yes, shall I open it?'

I was to report in a week's time to the WAAF Initial Training Camp at RAF Innsworth, Gloucester. 'Whoopee!' I shouted in that normally sedate office of the Scottish Provident Institution.

By now the remaining staff consisted of a few older men, a couple of staid women secretaries and the newly joined straight-from-school office junior. I had already notified the senior manager that I had volunteered but not told anyone else.

'I'm leaving next week. I'm going into the WAAF!'

'Good luck,' said the head of my department. 'I knew you'd be off before long! I envy you – wish I could go but they won't take me. My eyesight isn't good enough.' It was decided I could leave the next day to prepare for my new life.

That evening I said goodbye to the helpers at the YMCA with whom I worked during the Dunkirk days. The company secretary of the SPI handed me my final month's pay of £8, supplemented with holiday pay of £2, and a reference saying I was a diligent worker and the company wished me well in my Service life. I wondered whether it was going to be as interesting as I was expecting.

Twenty-four hours later I was on my way home, preparing to become a member of His Majesty's Services. King George VI had another wet-behind-the-ears recruit to train. One week to go.

Those seven days seemed endless. London was still being subjected to day and night bombing raids. More civilians killed, more houses destroyed. There were more ack-ack guns than ever and their sound was deafening. Greater numbers of fighter aircraft were now operating and I was able to recognise the outline of the Spitfires and Hurricanes as they harassed the intruders. Hitler was losing more of his bombers and their crews on every sortie. I felt proud of the RAF and thrilled to think I would very soon be part of it.

The last few days were spent in sorting out what clothes I would take with me and saying goodbye to the school friends who remained in the area. My parents did not say much as I made my preparations. I am sure they were a little apprehensive but they told me they were proud of my decision. My brother was nearly sixteen-years-old and was more worried about his Matriculation exams in the coming weeks.

On the morning before I left, a letter from George arrived. 'Good luck darling and let me know where you're posted. Bet you'll look good in uniform!' I was so glad to hear from him although I had no idea where he was. I carefully folded the letter and put it in my purse together with his photo in uniform.

That night I barely slept. I was so excited. I was dressed and ready before seven o'clock. My mother insisted I ate a large breakfast. 'You don't know when you'll have your next proper meal,' she said. By eight o'clock I was ready to go. I picked up my luggage and opened the front door.

There wasn't much in my rather battered leather suitcase; two pairs of pyjamas, a change of underclothes, a cardigan, my address book, notepaper and pen, a book to read on the journey and a packet of Spam sandwiches. I put my purse with two precious pounds in it into my pocket. I checked to see I had my railway warrant and letter of instructions and I turned to say goodbye.

My mother was looking anxious. 'Are you sure you'll be all right? Let me know you arrive safely, I'll be waiting for that phone call.' She handed me a pound note. 'Put that in your purse.' This was a large sum for her to give me. I knew my father only earned £4 a week as a cabinet maker. I tried to give it back but she insisted I kept it. 'You may need it,' she said and kissed me goodbye. 'Hurry now; you mustn't miss your train.' As I walked up the road on my way to the station, I took one last glance at the house and wondered when I would see my home again.

It was an early March day in 1941. The sun was shining but there was a chill in the air. I was wearing a blue jumper and a black skirt under my raincoat. I had decided to put on a strong pair of flat shoes as I thought I might have a lot of walking to do. At last I was on my way to join the WAAF, the Women's

THE NEW RECRUIT

Auxiliary Air Force to give it its full name. It seemed ages since I had volunteered, interviewed at the Air Ministry Recruiting Office and told to wait for my call-up papers. Finally the day had arrived to leave civilian life.

I made my way to the local suburban railway station, passing the familiar shops I had known since a child – past the *Little Lady's* sweet shop where I had once collected the cards from the penny bars of Nestlé chocolate I bought with my pocket money, past the Institute where we paid our monthly fee to belong to the Hospital Savings Association in case we were ever ill, and round the village green, which by now had been overtaken by suburban life.

I arrived at the station. It was the same line I had used daily to go to work in the City before the office evacuated to Woking. On this occasion I left the train at Kings Cross and took a bus to Paddington. I had orders to report to RAF Innsworth at Gloucester by 1300 hours. This was the first thing I had to get used to, using the twenty-four hour clock. It was to guide my way for the next five years.

Paddington Station was bustling with people, many of them in uniform. I could see service personnel everywhere, Army, Navy and Air Force. I passed Canadians, Australians, Poles and even a Free French airman, identified by their country's flash on their shoulder. All of them were carrying tin hats, gas masks and rifles as well as their kit. I wondered where they were off to – training camp like me or perhaps a war zone. I saw the red cap of a Military Policeman. I recognised it from the latest photo I had of George, who had recently been transferred to the Corps of Military Police.

I asked a porter which was the platform for the Gloucester train. 'Platform 14 over there,' he said, indicating to his left. 'It's already there waiting, you better get a move on.' I made my way to the man checking the tickets and showed him my travel warrant. Finding a Third Class carriage with an empty corner seat, I took out my book and sandwiches and placed the suitcase on the rack. My heart was thumping – what had I let myself in for? Thinking back, I am surprised; I did not feel anxious or bewildered, just excited. It was like opening the next page of a book I had always wanted to read.

The carriage was soon full, including several soldiers and two WAAF in their smart air force blue uniform who had jumped in at the last minute. I thought to myself: 'I hope I look as good as they do when I get my uniform', a consoling thought. The journey was to take two hours, and before long everyone was chatting with each other.

I tried to read my book but found myself constantly looking in the WAAF's direction. Eventually I plucked up courage and said: 'I am just on the way to join up, I'm going to RAF Innsworth.'

They both laughed and one said: 'You won't know what's hit you! Still, it only lasts a couple of weeks. After that you'll enjoy it.' They went on chatting together.

As the train drew into Gloucester station they pointed in the direction of an RAF sergeant standing on the platform. 'He's in charge of transport, go and report to him.'

I thanked them, reached for my suitcase and got out. As I approached he shouted: 'You for Innsworth?' I showed him my papers and he directed me to a transport lorry and told me to get in and wait. I pulled myself up with a rope over the tailboard and sat down on the bench.

There were six other girls there, all looking rather apprehensive. No-one said a word. The train pulled out, the sergeant lifted the tailboard and we set off. About fifteen minutes later the truck stopped. We were told to get out and check in at the Guard Room. We had arrived.

First impressions of Innsworth were daunting. It looked vast. The camp covered a huge area filled with rows and rows of grey Nissen huts interwoven with concrete paths. There was a large building at the far end and a huge parade ground in the middle. I could hear the shouts of command and could see rows of girls in squads marching up and down. I guessed I would soon be joining them.

Entering the large building, we were welcomed by a WAAF officer, who I later learnt was the Squadron Officer in charge. She handed us over to a sergeant who issued us with a large mug and *irons* – a knife, fork and spoon – and a linen bag to keep them in. We were told to take these with us whenever we went for meals to the Mess. We were then taken to one of the Nissen huts and handed over to the hut corporal, a tall bossy girl with a strong North Country accent.

'I'm Corporal Stevens and I'm in charge of this hut. If there is anything you need to know, you must come and ask me. You will call me Corporal. You are in hut seven and don't forget it,' she barked. Seven was my lucky number, so that was easy to remember. We were each allocated a metal bed and told that was our space. There were thirty beds arranged against the two side walls.

On each bed there were three individual square pads piled on top of each other called *biscuits*. They were brown, solid and covered in a thick rough fabric. On top of these was the bedding, which consisted of two brown blankets, two white cotton sheets folded neatly, a thin limp pillow without a pillowcase, all wrapped in another blanket.

The corporal told us this was how we had to stack the bedding every morning, and we could not make up the beds before 1700 hours. 'That's five o'clock,' I reminded myself. We each had a locker beside the bed and a small mat. Behind the bed was a hook to hang our uniform, no hangers provided! This was to be my home for the next fortnight. So far I had not had time to see who I was to share this with for the next two weeks.

The huts were hardly homely. They were warmed by an iron stove with a chimney that went out through the roof. The floor was bare. As we would be away from the huts all day, we were told not to light the fires before 1700 hours. This seemed to be the magic hour for everything. We later found out that it took two hours to heat up and then the temperature became hot and steamy. But during the early hours as the stove went out we would wake up to a miserably cold hut.

At the far end was the Corporal's room. We were then taken to the ablutions, which were shared by several huts of new recruits. This was another word I had to learn. Ablutions were in a hut quite a distance from ours with four baths, a row of wash basins and toilets and a very cold concrete floor. I was glad I had been a Girl Guide and used to roughing things at camp since it looked as if life would be a little hard for the coming days.

Marching, Saluting & Posting

The other six girls who were in the transport with me were allocated beds opposite and next to mine. So far we had barely spoken, only to give our names and show our identity cards. As we were all new recruits and going through the ordeal together I decided it was time we got to know each other. I said: 'I'm Eileen. Since we are going to be together for some time, we'd better introduce ourselves.'

A tall, dark-haired girl immediately answered: 'I'm Peggy and this is Jean,' pointing to the fair-haired girl next to her, 'We both come from Devon.' This broke the ice and before long, we had all introduced ourselves. A couple of girls were from Lancashire with strong local accents. Another very shy girl whispered: 'I'm Doreen and I live in Southampton.' The last one, very obviously a Cockney, said her name was Hettie. We chatted together for about half an hour, just enough time to put our belongings in our locker before Corporal Stevens returned.

'Right, bring your irons and get something to eat in the Mess. It's over there.' She pointed to a large hut at the end of the parade ground. 'When you've finished report to the Medical HQ. Then return to your hut.' She marshalled us outside and called to four other girls from the other end of the hut to join us. 'Fall in. You will march over there. I hope no-one is wearing high heels.' She glanced disapprovingly at one girl's very elegant but unsuitable shoes. 'Get into line, three abreast, hurry up.'

The eleven of us were sorted into lines of three with the odd two sandwiched in the middle. 'Left, right, left, right,' she shouted. 'As usual someone doesn't know their right foot from their left. Sort yourself out, you at the back.' Thank goodness it wasn't me. I'd been used to marching in the Girl Guides but it seemed an awfully long way. I was glad I had my flat shoes on.

In the Mess we found masses of long wooden tables. At the far end four WAAF cooks were serving something that looked like a stew. They piled up our metal plates and pointed to dishes of potatoes, cabbage and parsnips. 'Help yourselves, the bread's at the end.' We sat together at one of the tables and looked at the stew. I never did identify the meat.

This was my first Service meal and very different from home cooking! But I was so hungry, it was soon all gone. A stodgy pudding was followed by a mug of very strong tea, something I would never have drunk at home. Whilst we were eating, we began talking about where we came from and what we did before we joined up.

I soon realised we were a very mixed bunch, with varying backgrounds and levels of education. I wondered what trade we would all end up doing and where we would be posted. We would probably never see each other again after these two weeks of close contact; ships that pass in the night, except it would take a fortnight.

Twenty minutes later, Corporal Stevens returned: "Get cracking and line up in threes outside. Time for your medical and FFI, then your injections.' At that, one of the girls cried out: 'Oh no!' The Corporal gave her a disapproving glance and went on: 'Then you will go to Equipment for your uniforms.'

'What's FFI?' the Cockney girl asked.

'Free from infection. We check you don't have nits, and if you do, we treat your hair with paraffin to kill them off! Then you are isolated for three days so you don't infect anyone else.'

'Gawd 'elp us!' said Hettie. I looked around at the others, wondering if any of our group would have to undergo that humiliation.

The next hour was frenetic, rushing from one section to the other, as well as suffering a triple injection against typhoid, paratyphoid, cholera and goodness knows what else. I was glad to find we had all passed the FFI inspection without any problem. I didn't fancy sharing the hut with nits. The RAF medic only gave us a cursory examination, as I imagine we had all had a full medical at our first interview on volunteering.

Then we were marched to Equipment. The RAF sergeant looked us up and down and shouted to one of the airwomen: 'This one's size 12 and the next 18.' It seemed like a lot of guesswork but amazingly, in most cases he wasn't far wrong.

We were first issued with a kitbag and the rest of our future uniform gradually arrived; one greatcoat, one air force blue cardigan, two skirts and two tunics, three air force blue shirts, a tie and three collars for which we were told we had to provide the studs ourselves. After that we were given two pairs of heavy black shoes, three pairs of thick grey lisle stockings, two scratchy vests, one white suspender belt, two white cotton bras and two pairs of the famous "blackouts," voluminous black knickers in a heavy woollen fabric. These were also known as passion killers! Then came the final garment, a khaki groundsheet to be used as a raincoat. It seemed we had to provide our own sleepwear.

We were given two shoe brushes and a metal button stick – a contraption to slide behind our buttons so that when we polished them daily, the metal polish would not soil the uniform. We had to buy the metal polish and shoe-polish ourselves. There was also a tin hat and a service gas mask, much more substantial than the one issued to civilians. The final item was a *housewife*, pronounced *hussif* – a heavy cotton pouch containing needles, pins, a pair of scissors and grey and white cotton. All a girl would need to change from a civilian to an airwoman.

We struggled to cram all this into our kitbags. 'Right, back to the hut girls and sort yourselves out,' said the ever-present Corporal. 'You will have to send your civilian clothes home. You will always travel in uniform. Any questions?'

'Yes Corporal,' I ventured. 'Is it possible to make a phone call?'

She pointed to the other end of the building. 'The phone's there. Right, fall in. Quick march!'

Still out of step we marched back to the hut, struggling with our kitbags. Hettie, who was marching alongside me, whispered: 'You won't get me wearing those black bloomers!'

We found Hut Seven full of more WAAF already in their uniforms. They looked at us in a superior way. We were now the new arrivals. They had three days experience! But it was not long before we were all talking together, asking questions and trying to feel less strange. It was a funny feeling being in a hut with twenty-nine other women. Fortunately, as it was past 1700 hours, the fires had already been lit and the hut was feeling much warmer.

Even after this short time several of the girls were already making new friends. The two girls from Devon were in the beds alongside mine and after we had sorted and tried on our uniforms we sat on our beds and chatted. They both came from Totnes and had been at school together. Ann had worked as a clerk in an estate agent's office and Jean was a typist in the council offices.

'We both want to go into admin,' Peggy told me. 'We are used to office work. Hope we can stay together.' Most didn't have any idea what they would be doing. I seemed the only one who had been allocated a definite trade.

'I am going to be a Clerk Special Duties'.

'What's that?' they asked.

'I've no idea, but you have to be good at maths, I think.'

There was a lot of laughter as we tried on our uniforms, especially when Cockney Hettie paraded in her blackouts. I could see she was going to keep us amused. 'If anyone's uniform really doesn't fit then you must take it back to Equipment and have it changed,' said Corporal Stevens. Amazingly there was only one wrong size. Sheila from Surrey had a greatcoat which swallowed her. 'Right, go back and change it now.' Sheila looked terrified. I guess she was frightened to face the RAF sergeant.

One more trek to the Mess for tea, consisting of thick corned beef sandwiches, a slice of *yellow peril* – a solid lump of indigestible Madeira cake – and more strong tea from the urn, then it was time to turn in. I managed to escape for a quick phone call home to say I had arrived safely. I couldn't talk for more than a couple of minutes as there was a long queue waiting, all eager to report home.

I just had time to ask my father to send me a bath plug. "What on earth do you want that for? Are you going to be a plumber?'

'No,' I explained 'I have seen the baths and none of them have plugs in them, so I thought it would be a good idea if I had one of my own!' I could hear him laughing.

By the time I returned to the hut every bed was taken. We new ones struggled to make our beds. We were all tired but I for one was not so sure whether I would manage to sleep. Already one of the girls was tearful and homesick. I just felt excited. I remember how strange it all seemed that first night. Sleep was fitful; the three biscuits put together to form a mattress kept coming apart. I thought there must be a better way to get round this problem but that would be for tomorrow. Then I fell asleep.

We had been warned there would be an early morning alarm call and sure enough at 0600 hours a klaxon sounded and a hut of sleepy new WAAF woke to another day. After a dash to the ablution hut and a chilly wash we put on our new uniforms. Somehow it made all us all feel different. We held our heads high in pride at belonging to the RAF.

A swift breakfast, then we were marshalled on to the parade ground by Corporal Stevens and handed over to an RAF sergeant. For the next two hours we were marched up and down until our feet ached. We right dressed, we about turned, we stood to attention and we stood at ease. We didn't all turn the right way or stop quickly enough, so there were collisions and trip-ups and a lot of sarcastic comments from our instructor. But finally we began to get it right. We were released for a break and then told to run at the double back to the main building for a lecture. And so it went on for two weeks.

We learnt about venereal diseases, a completely new subject to several of us, but not all. We were taught how to salute – the longest way up and the shortest way down. We heard about the history of the Royal Air Force, how it was formed in World War One as the Royal Flying Corps. We had to learn the different ranks of officers, how to recognise them and never to pass one, male or female, without saluting.

As each day followed the last, we ate, we slept, we marched. We learnt about daily routine orders and what would happen if we disobeyed an order. We were interviewed individually by a group of psychologists, testing our aptitude for whatever trade we were allocated. There was a special test for vision to check we were not colour-blind. Each evening we would return to our huts exhausted but on the whole delighted we had survived another day. On the fifth day two of our hut members never returned after one session. We assumed they had failed some vital test.

One evening whilst in the ablution hut, I heard some strange groaning sounds. To my dismay I found a newly arrived recruit lying on the floor of one of the toilets, writhing in agony. 'I'm having a baby!' she shrieked, 'Help me, get someone quick.' I had no idea what to do so I called for Corporal Stevens and she came to the rescue.

I realised what a very sheltered life I had lived until then. Already from the conversations of others in the hut, I could see how innocent my upbringing had been. There were girls from all kinds of backgrounds, both tragic and doubtful. Hettie boasted she had been a prostitute. Another had been abandoned and brought up in an orphanage. How lucky I had been to have a wonderful supportive family and the chance of a good education! In those few days I learnt a lot about life.

It was almost our final day at Innsworth. The rag-taggle bunch of girls could now march well, were more disciplined and were now part of His Majesty's Royal Air Force. It was time to find out where we were to be posted. We were called in one by one. I learnt that I was confirmed as a Clerk Special Duties and had to report to a unit at Leighton Buzzard for special training. I was the only one going there.

Of our original seven new recruits, one had failed to pass the course, two were to become cooks, one a driver, and the two Devon girls were both going for admin training as they had wished. Hettie the prostitute was one of the girls to be trained as a cook. I asked her: 'What made you decide to join up?'

Her answer was short and to the point: 'I got fed up with men!'

We received our travelling instructions and rail warrants. We attended our first pay parade. This was a new procedure we had to learn. It would happen every two weeks. We lined up and as our names were called we marched forward to the paymaster, called out our number and name – '445020 Le Croissette' – and saluted. The money was then counted out into our hand and we saluted again. We received two-thirds of an airman's pay. It was not very much, one shilling and eight pence a day (8p in today's money).

There was one more talk by the Squadron Officer in charge who wished us well in our future trades. Then we showed off our newly acquired marching skills in the Passing Out Parade. The last evening was spent packing our belongings and cleaning the hut and then a final night's sleep.

Learning the Secret

It was Friday morning. The klaxon sounded and we jumped out of our beds, dressed, folded our bedding – wrapping up the three *biscuits* for the last time. After breakfast, with our kit packed, we marched to the guardroom where the lorry was waiting. Once more we grabbed the rope and heaved ourselves into the RAF transport. Our kit was thrown in after us and piled up on the floor. We squeezed on to the two long bench seats, feeling particularly uncomfortable with our tin hats pushing into our backs and our gas mask case over our shoulder.

I was excited, knowing that at last I was going to find out what Clerk Special Duties meant. At that stage I still had no idea but somehow envisaged sitting in an office juggling with figures. How wrong I was!

At the end of our initial training we had been given a forty-eight hour pass and told we had to report to our next training unit before 1700 hours on Sunday. Several of us were heading home to London so we found an empty carriage at Gloucester station and compared notes. Two were going to RAF Bridgenorth for training in admin; others were off to various parts of Britain as cooks and drivers. My destination was to be RAF Leighton Buzzard in Bedfordshire.

We separated in London, knowing we would probably never meet again after sharing two weeks together in very close proximity and suffering numerous indignities together. Despite our disparate backgrounds, we had formed a bond. I knew Hettie would cope whatever she did but I wondered about some of the others.

Taking the Piccadilly tube to Wood Green felt very different from the many other times I had travelled on this line. People looked at me differently. Girls who had joined the ATS, our army equivalent, often found the public hostile, looking on them as a threat since they would be sharing life with their husbands and boyfriends. I never encountered any animosity. Perhaps it was due to the agonies of the Blitz and the respect the public had for the fighter pilots who fought so hard to protect them.

My parents were delighted to see me home for the first time in my uniform, although it was only a brief visit. Even my brother said I looked smart. I was looking forward to some home cooking. The time went quickly. I managed to see a few friends. Then it was Sunday, the day I was to leave for my next training camp.

My mother must have saved their meagre rations for the occasion because we had a wonderful traditional Sunday lunch. Her Yorkshire pudding must have used their egg ration for the month and their meat ration too must have gone to provide the joint of beef. I hoped they would not go hungry in the coming days as I knew things were difficult and food was short.

It was great to be home but I was anxious to get on with my training. About an hour after that special meal, I was on my way back to London to catch a train to Leighton Buzzard. My mother was less anxious this time as I left. 'Good luck,' she said as she hugged me tightly.

I had remembered to pack a notebook as I was sure there would be a lot to learn. I was used to taking notes, but what would it be about? It was around 1800 hours on that April Sunday evening as I alighted from the train at my final destination and looked for any signs of an RAF transport. Sure enough, there was the usual lorry waiting outside the station. A few more WAAF, a couple of airmen and I once more did the *rope trick*, joining five other passengers already in the back. 'Another train to wait for and then we'll be off,' the driver called out to us. Half an hour later, two more airmen joined us and we were on the road.

We drove through the town and out into the country. We passed several farms and a few cottages before we drew up outside the camp. Reporting as usual to the guardroom, I noticed that everywhere was highly camouflaged. The buildings were covered by a heavy green fabric, giving the impression that it was part of the countryside. The material matched the colour of the fields and had outlines of trees painted over it. I wondered what was so important here to receive this treatment.

Several of my fellow WAAF were as puzzled as I was. I guessed they too were new. Reporting to the duty officer, we were told we would be accommodated in the Workhouse! This was a building within walking distance and not quite as unpleasant as the name suggested. We were taken there, allotted beds, once again equipped with the ubiquitous biscuits, and told to get a meal and then report back to the main building.

We quickly dumped our kit and made our way over to the Mess where we were offered once more the *yellow peril* cake" – obviously a mass purchase by the RAF – washed down by the customary strong cup of tea. I couldn't face the doorstep sandwiches on offer after my mother's home cooking. As we ate I found out we were all destined to be Clerks SD. Now I would learn what it meant.

Back in the main building we were directed to the new intake briefing room. There were about thirty of us, mostly WAAF but we noticed a few airmen who all seemed to be quite a bit older than us. A Wing Commander, heavily bemedalled, arrived and addressed us.

'You are about to become part of a very important branch of the Royal Air Force, vital for the defence of Great Britain.' There was a general intake of breath and we all seemed to straighten ourselves and become more attentive.

'Before you start any further training, because of its highly secret nature, you are compelled to sign the Official Secrets Act. This Act demands that you never pass on information you may gather during your training or your future duties, since it would endanger the security of our nation.' He looked serious. 'Anyone who refuses to sign will leave this room instantly and will be returned to their previous camp, to be directed to other duties. I will call your name and you will each come up and sign the necessary form. Any questions?' Nobody said a word. I imagine we were all too surprised.

In turn we made our way to the table and signed this important document. I wondered what we were going to learn that was so secret. The Wing Commander left with his final word: 'Good luck and work hard.' The duty RAF Sergeant took over. 'Dismiss and report here tomorrow at 0800 hours.'

Returning to our hut, we discussed what could it be that we were to be a part of. 'Do you think we're going to be spies?' someone asked.

'Course not, we're only airwomen and the lowest rank there is!' It was hard to sleep that night. It seemed only a few hours later when the 0600 hours wake-up call sounded. We dressed, made our way to the Mess for breakfast and then twenty-odd excited young women reported to the Briefing Room.

This time a WAAF Flight Officer addressed us. 'You will all be working as part of the RDF chain. RDF means range and direction finding.' She went on to explain how the air defence of Britain depended on this elaborate warning system. She told us how a chain of coastal RDF stations picked up signals from approaching aircraft. This information was reported to a Filter Room where the information was plotted on a General Situations Map, corrected, collated and identified. This was then passed on in its refined form to various Group and Sector Operations Rooms and to the Observer Corps. It would be used to direct fighter interceptions, give air raid warnings, assist rescue operations and instruct army gun crews for gun-laying and firing.

We would be allotted to one of three different trades; RDF (later renamed Radar) Operator, Filter Room Plotter or Operations Room Plotter. She read out each name and the trade for which they would receive training. When my name was called, she said: 'Filter Plotter.'

We were separated into three groups. I noticed that most of the airmen were in the Radar operators group with three of the WAAF. There were only six Filter Plotters and the remainder were sent to the Operations Room group.

'You will all attend the first two days' lectures,' said the Flight Officer. 'These cover how the system works; you will learn about radio waves, goniometers and various other technical details. Then you will separate and go to different areas, learning the specific skills needed for your individual tasks. Wait here for your first lecture.' She handed over to a civilian. He announced he was a scientist and he would explain the rudiments of RDF.

I had only studied Physics up to General Schools level so I hoped I would be able to understand. At first the technical details were hard to grasp. We were given the analogy that the system worked in the same way as if we threw a pebble into a lake. The ripples would move outwards and if they hit an obstacle, they would return towards us. This was how radio waves behaved when they hit a metal surface – an approaching aircraft in this case. The signal would appear as an echo on a linear trace on the cathode ray tube and give warning of a possible enemy raid. At this stage the scientist did not go into too much detail.

Over the next two days we heard of Watson Watts' early experiments at the Radio Research Station at Datchet in the early 1930s, tracking thunderstorms by radio and ionospheric ranging by pulse transmission – how he had gone on to evolve the present system which had been put into operation from the first days of war, and that the work we were training for was part of the chain of advance warning based on this.

We heard how the Radar operators and plotters at the coastal stations converted these signals into an estimated range, height and direction of the detected aircraft, as well as indicating if the Identification Friend or Foe (IFF) signal was being shown. This information was sent in the form of a map position, via telephone lines to the Filter Room, where the Filter Plotter would display counters indicating all the information received from each coastal station on the large gridded map table. This would be refined by Filterer Officers, who would instantly recalculate the correct position, number of aircraft and height, showing direction with an arrow. Each track would be numbered, identified and constantly reassessed in the Filter Room.

It was emphasised that speed was of the essence. The aircraft were constantly moving and information needed to be updated at speed. The tracks would be numbered and identified by the Filter Room Controller with the help of the Movements Liaison section who knew all movements of friendly aircraft. They together with a supervising Filter Officer would be situated on a balcony above.

The updated information would constantly be *told* or passed on by the tellers to the Operations Room and all who needed to know. This included Group and Sector Operations who initiated air raid warnings and interception actions, and also the Royal Observer Corps who would take over the tracking over land. At this stage in its development Radar suffered interference, known as ground rays, from metal installations and buildings when used over land. We were mesmerised.

We didn't understand everything that first day but we realised we would be taking part in something vital to the defence of our country and I am sure we all felt proud. I just hoped I would be good enough to do my job properly.

The second day there were more lectures. We were shown films of Radar stations with their four enormous steel pylons bearing the curtain array of transmitting aerials and the single shorter wooden receiver pylon. We saw the Radar operators sitting in front of the screen – a plain cathode ray tube just like a TV monitor with a single line of light across it, showing a pulsating echo when a response was received. We saw the Operations Room with its large table and the girls around it wearing headsets and moving counters and markers with a long pole. It all seemed quite peaceful and organised.

Finally we were shown a film of the Filter Room at Fighter Command, which covered the defence of the vital south coast and Thames Estuary. 'That's where I may be one day,' I thought.

In complete contrast to the calm of the Operations Room, the Filter Room was a hive of activity; girls crowded around the table placing and removing many counters; officers having to push their way through them to put down their arrows or change the information on the metal raid plaques. They looked up to the balcony, answering questions from the officers above. There was constant movement. It looked like chaos but it worked. From the balcony the Controller, a senior RAF officer, was shouting instructions, identifying aircraft, always on the alert.

We learnt how few aircraft we had at the beginning of the war, and how impossible it would have been to have them in the air constantly patrolling on the lookout for enemy aircraft. We were told how too few trained fighter pilots there were, as well as a shortage of fuel for the planes. We realised that without Radar the invasion of Britain could well happen.

The day ended. 'Tomorrow you will separate for your specialised training,' the lecturer said as he left the room. 'Good luck!' We were exhausted with all the new knowledge but thrilled to learn how Britain's scientists had prepared this great weapon of defence. I now knew the secret my school friend could not tell me.

Reporting next morning to the training room for Filter Plotters I found there would be ten of us undergoing training there, all young women between nineteen and twenty-four years of age. The room was large, almost completely taken over by an oddly shaped table. Looking at it more closely I could see that it followed the shape of the coastline from the north of Norfolk to the Isle of Wight. As well as part of the inland area behind the coast, it extended over the English Channel and part of the North Sea and continued over the coast of Holland, Belgium and France. The table was divided into large squares, each bearing two capital letters.

The Flight Sergeant ordered us to take our places at any of the chairs around it, to await the arrival of Squadron Leader Mann who would be instructing us. In front of each place was a headset and lead. A few minutes later we were told to stand to attention as he entered the room. Seated once more, we began our first lesson on plotting.

Squadron Leader Mann was a *wingless wonder*, the term given to officers who were not aircrew. He was about forty-years-old and had been enrolled from the group of scientific observers who had worked closely with RDF from the early days. He began: 'This room is an exact copy of the 11 Group Filter Room sited at Fighter Command headquarters at Stanmore. That is where the Battle of Britain was played out.'

He explained that it was the busiest of the seven Filter rooms and guarded the area experiencing most enemy activity. 'You will now learn how the work of Plotters was vital in that battle.' He emphasised that the job we would be doing was of critical importance for the defence of Britain and that we must be quick and accurate at all times.

He told us that the whole of Britain, the sea and countries surrounding it were mapped in this same way, in squares identified with two letters, starting with AA to AB and moving through the alphabet. Each place where we were seated was connected to a different Chain Home RDF station. All positions plotted on the table would be referred to by two letters and four figures, for example Victor Willie 5-3.7-4. To find the position we would measure each square as in decimals, east to west and north to south, so the number would signify 5.3 across and 7.4 down.

He gave us a list to learn of the RAF code names for each letter – Apple, Beer, Charlie, Dog and so on. These designations were used in the RAF throughout the war. We were told we had to learn these names at once as we would use them all the time. It was the Americans who introduced the code names now used such as Alpha, Foxtrot, Tango. But I use the original names to this day since they had become part of me from that first day of training.

We were given a box of counters. Each station was allocated a different colour. Painted on the map table, there were a series of arcs radiating from each station. These were in the station's colour and were ten miles apart. I found that my position was connected to Rye on the south coast, and green was my colour.

I noticed that there were several different shapes amongst the counters. This was our next lesson. Circles were used to show the position, triangles the estimated number of aircraft, and squares the estimated height. In addition there were rectangles marked IFF short for Identification Friend or Foe; a friendly aircraft: and others BIF, a Mayday code giving warning that the aircraft was in distress.

Putting on our headsets and plugging in the lead, we made contact with our mock station. For a while we were told just to listen. A man's voice announced: "New track, Victor Willie 9-1, 4-3, 15 plus at 20, showing IFF.' At first it made no sense, but after listening for a few minutes I was able to understand the instructions. Squadron Leader Mann emphasised that we must be accurate and fast. There was no time for misunderstandings. For this reason, all those chosen as either plotters or tellers had to speak clearly with no regional accent.

A WAAF sergeant sitting at one of the stations demonstrated how to display the plots but first she pointed out they each bore a number from one to five. This number would indicate the time the plot was put down. The counter used had to relate to the period indicated by the Sector Clock on the wall. After a certain period out-of-time plots had to be removed to avoid confusion. It was explained that the Filterer Officer, when correcting the position of a raid, needed to collate information from several stations and the information from all sources must be equally up-to-date. It was getting more and more complicated. Would I ever learn all these procedures?

'Right,' said the Squadron Leader, 'That's enough for this morning. Go for your lunch. When you return, you will do the plotting.'

As we left, Joan White, who had sat next to me, said: 'I'm sure I'll never be able to do this.'

I did my best to encourage her: 'We're all finding it difficult, but I'm sure it will make sense before long.' As we ate our lunch, everyone admitted it was hard to take it all in, but we agreed it was certainly better than working in the kitchen or driving a truck.

Back from lunch, plugged into our stations, we had our first effort at plotting the information we received. At first we were clumsy and very slow – fiddling in the box to find the right counter, using the wrong number, asking the voice on the phone to repeat the instructions. The sergeant supervising our efforts was calm and reassuring. He did his best to encourage us. 'Just take your time; you'll soon get the hang of it.'

As the afternoon wore on I felt I was getting quicker at putting down the right counters. All of us were improving. The table was now covered with coloured counters and things began to take shape. I was getting the hang of it. When we were told: 'That's enough for today,' although mentally exhausted, we were feeling pleased with our efforts.

Back in the hut we were excited but slightly overawed. We agreed we felt apprehensive as to whether we would ever be fast enough. 'We're really going to do something important, aren't we?' said Joan.

We sat on our beds and discussed what we had learnt. As we talked we found that some of the things we had not understood, others could help with. By the time we had talked over our difficulties we felt more confident to face the next day's tuition. That night we slept soundly.

The following morning Sergeant Jones explained how the information we were plotting was used. 'As soon as the first plot on a new track appears, the Filterer Officer will place a halma down and call to the Raid Orderly for a magnetised metal plaque giving the next raid number.'

'What's a halma?' someone asked. He held one up and I recognised it as a piece from a childhood board game, a small cone-shaped object with a tiny sphere on the top.

He continued describing the procedure. When a second plot appeared, an arrow was placed indicating the direction. As the Radar operator gave each new piece of information, the Filterer Officer would ask the Raid Orderly to add metal numbers, indicating number of aircraft and height, to the raid plaque. We could see that if a second station picked up a signal from the same aircraft, then by intersecting the arcs, a corrected position could be found.

As the session closed the instructor reminded us: 'It is essential that as Plotters, you always keep the information up-to-date. You must work fast because any time lag when enemy aircraft are approaching would cause a delay in giving air raid warnings and initiating fighter interceptions.

'When there is a Mayday, the S.O.S signal, that's Broad IF, this takes priority,' he emphasised. 'Any delay means Air Sea Rescue might not get there in time. People's lives depend on you.' I realised then that when I said I was good at maths, this was one of the key elements for working in the Filter Room.

Each day there was more to learn about procedures. We were shown how raids were identified as friendly, doubtful or hostile, how friendly aircraft would be divided into Fighter, Bomber, Coastal Command or Army Co-operation. We learnt that on the balcony above the Filter Room table would be a team of Movement Liaison personnel who received information of all known RAF operations, and how the Filter Room Controller would use this to identify the tracks. We were shown how our *cleaned up* or filtered information was passed on by tellers, also seated on the balcony, to all who needed to know – Group and Sector Operations Rooms, Observer Corps, Air Raid Warning centres, Royal Artillery anti-aircraft gun sites, Air Sea Rescue. There was even a line to Churchill's War Room.

We learned that the Filter Room was the focal point of intelligence on enemy air activity. Information from Radar station, Y service, Bletchley and military intelligence were all co-ordinated by the Filter Room into a real time picture of the battle.

This information went to AA guns, civil defence, air raid warnings and Search and Rescue as well as fighter squadrons.

Some days we were given more technical lectures on how radio waves worked and shown how some stations might receive more accurate information than others. We were told that the Chain Home stations were sited on high ground to give the best coverage. New means of detection were constantly being found and improved Radar coverage developed. We must be prepared to adapt to new methods as these techniques were added.

During those twelve days we became more proficient, except for one girl who had already been there a week before us but who could not master it at all. By the fifth day she failed to appear. She had been taken off Special Duties and sent back to RAF Innsworth but, as she had signed the Official Secrets Act, she would be posted to one of the Operations Rooms and trained as a telephone operator.

Despite being tired at the end of each day, we managed to find the energy to visit the NAAFI for a bit of relaxation and there was even a dance organised for us on the first Saturday evening with a live RAF band. A crowd of airmen from a nearby operational fighter station had been invited to partner us. We were warned not to discuss our training with anyone. That evening we forgot everything about plotting and relaxed and danced the night away.

On the following Friday our period of training was almost over. We had a short written test and then a final plotting session. That afternoon Squadron Leader Mann told us that we had all passed and would now be sent out to one of the seven Filter Rooms covering the whole of Britain and Northern Ireland, from the Shetlands to Lands End. Initially no-one would be sent to

Fighter Command Headquarters at Stanmore, the area with most activity. 'You must first prove you are fast and accurate before you go there, but I am sure some of you will get there one day. I wish you well and don't forget all I have told you.'

So this intense fortnight's instruction was over. We would now learn where we were to be posted. To my delight, I heard I was being sent to 10 Group RAF Rudloe Manor, very near Bath where my aunt and uncle lived, the parents of my cousin Eric Padfield whose death had spurred me on to join the WAAF. I was told that it was the next busiest Filter Room to Stanmore. I couldn't wait to get there.

Operation Plotter

The journey to my new posting took me via Paddington and a Great Western train to Bath. It was a damp April morning, no time to spend a night at home. Once more in London I could see the damage from the bombing. Londoners were still suffering. As the train left Paddington station we passed devastated streets, houses with their roofs torn off, whole walls missing, looking like dolls' houses open to the public gaze.

Soon we reached the outskirts of the city where the damage was less and finally we were travelling through the green and peaceful countryside of Wiltshire before approaching the beautiful city of Bath. Trailing my kitbag behind me, I made for the RAF Transport Office to learn there was a truck about to leave for Rudloe Manor. I joined several other airmen and airwomen in the back and off we went along the A4 into the country. They all seemed to know each other. I definitely felt like the new girl.

Passing the village of Box, we turned into the camp. I could see it overlooked a deep valley, with an airfield on the ridge on the other side. This was RAF Colerne where there was a squadron of Polish and Czech pilots in residence. After reporting to the guardroom, I was taken to the Duty Admin Officer who was to brief me. Filter Room Plotters did not sleep on camp but were billeted in nearby villages. I was to go to Corsham, a lovely Wiltshire village complete with a Lord of the Manor in his beautiful manor house. In the billet I would be sharing a room with another WAAF Plotter.

The duty sergeant then took over to guide me through my first experience of 10 Group Filter Room. To my surprise I was taken underground. As we were a vital part of the defence chain we had to be protected. There were vast caves under the camp extending in many directions. Later I learnt many of our national treasures were stored there throughout the war to protect them from bomb damage. In fact, just 100 feet below the rolling Wiltshire countryside are mile upon mile of tunnels, an amazing labyrinth of long forgotten military sites.

We descended in a lift. Now I had my first view of where I would spend many future hours. Sometimes it would be very busy and sometimes, when the weather was bad and there was no flying, there would be long periods of boredom and cold. The set-up in this underground room was similar to that of the training room at Leighton Buzzard – a large map table, surrounded by airwomen and a couple of airmen wearing headsets, all busy talking on telephones. Above them on the balcony, I recognised a familiar layout; there was the Controller, a RAF Squadron Leader, and a WAAF Flight Officer sitting next to him. Behind was the Movement Liaison team and on a small jutting-out section the two WAAF tellers. There was also an Army officer who I was told was the Air Raid Warnings Liaison Officer.

The whole room was buzzing, the noise level so high that it was difficult to distinguish what everyone was saying. The plotters were repeating their grid positions as they stretched across the table and laid down their counters. From the balcony, the Controller called out: 'Make track 140 a hostile and 142 a fighter.' The Raid Orderly was handing the next metal plaque with its raid number at the command of the Filterer Officer. On the wall was the Sector Clock. It was thrilling to see the reality of how Radar information was being used in real time.

So much was happening it was impossible to assimilate it all. I could see the area covered by 10 Group Filter Room overlapped the Isle of Wight with that of 11 Group at Stanmore. It continued westwards along the coast to Lands End and then to north Wales and the Cheshire border, overlapping 9 Group Filter Room coverage at RAF Barton Hall near Preston. I was seeing how the Chain Home coverage was protecting our coasts.

It was now early evening. The Watch Sergeant took me aside and explained I would be joining this watch, C Watch, for future duties. There were four Filter watch crews and the day was split into three different watch periods, from 0800 to 1600 hours, 1600 hours to midnight, and midnight to 0800 hours. I would not work the same time every day but would move on one session. This meant my sleep pattern would change daily. However, when any watch was sent on leave – 'two weeks a year, if you are lucky' – the schedule changed to a three watch basis and little free time.

I would be picked up from my billet an hour before the watch started, to get a meal at the base. If I went off camp during off-duty periods, I had to report back in time for duty – 'No exceptions', warned the Sergeant. 'Otherwise you'll be put on a charge.' This meant a punishment of extra duties on the camp. She reminded me there would be a kit inspection every week and I would have to lay out my kit in the prescribed manner on my bed. As we were on special duties, we would not have to attend church parade or do any PT or marching exercises. This was a bonus, although I could see living off camp and having to rely on transport might waste a lot of our spare time.

OPERATION PLOTTER

I was put under the supervision of the Watch Corporal on one of the Radar stations to see if I could cope. I remember the name of that station was Downderry. It was a small coastal village, west of Plymouth and near Torpoint. Of course I was nervous, but as there was little activity in the area at the time I was gradually able to get the feel of it. I worked for the rest of the watch, still under supervision, and was told that next time on duty, I would be given a station of my own.

There was a male operator on duty on the Downderry phone that first time. He spoke clearly but quite fast. In the slack periods, I noticed the other Plotters were chatting to their unknown voices on the end of the line. So I joined in and explained to my Radar operator that this was my very first watch. From then on he went out of his way to help me.

These conversations with the Radar ops were called *binding* and many friendships had been forged that way, some ending in marriage. I realised early on that it was essential to build a rapport in order to speed up reporting. I remembered how it had been impressed upon us that speed and accuracy were essential to give the maximum warning of the approach of enemy aircraft, thus ensuring fast interception by our fighters.

When the watch ended I was introduced to the girl I was to share the billet with. Her name was Ruth Hibberd. She seemed friendly and said: 'Don't worry, I'll show you the ropes, ask me if there is anything you want to know and I'll give you the gen.' The watch ended at midnight. It had been a long day. On going up to the surface by lift and then straight to the Mess for supper, I realised that as well as adjusting to new sleep patterns, meals would also be at odd times. I hoped I would be able to cope.

Most of C Watch was also billeted in Corsham and the transport dropped us off en route. Our house was almost the last. I barely registered where it was that first night. It was one o'clock in the morning. We crept upstairs and I fell into bed, exhausted but elated. I had just plotted some Nazi bombers that were aiming to attack the docks at Plymouth and a section of intercepting RAF fighters. At the time they were counters on a table, but before I fell asleep I realised they were real aircrew in real aircraft, one side intent on destruction and the other on prevention.

The following morning I found that I was billeted in a large detached house with a lovely garden looking out over fields. I met the owners, Mr and Mrs Clarke, who informed me they owned the local coal merchants. I was glad to hear this as it meant the house would always be warm! They said I could use the kitchen during the day when they were absent and make my own meals but I must bring my own food from the camp as their rations were very short. Mrs. Clarke said I could also use the garden if I wished. Ruth told me they were very pleasant people but she never saw much of them. So far, so good.

Ruth and I caught the transport at a central spot in the village the next morning, in time for a late breakfast in the Mess. I spent the afternoon finding out about camp facilities. I located the NAAFI, a vital place where we could buy small items like toothpaste, notepaper, postage stamps, and where coffee, tea and snacks were available. It was also where any entertainment on the camp took place.

I returned to Corsham in the late afternoon intending to have a few hours rest before facing my first midnight watch. It was impossible to sleep and I realised that these odd sleep patterns would be one of the most difficult aspects of watch-keeping that I would have to adjust to.

That first eight-hour night watch was hard. I had to fight the desire to sleep. I was placed on a station with little activity until the dawn patrols went out. It became very cold in the early hours since both heating and air conditioning were fairly primitive. We were allowed two fifteen-minute breaks for tea and a sandwich in a canteen down in the depths of the quarry. I survived my first night.

Returning to the billet, I tried to sleep during the daylight hours but found it almost impossible. Ruth told me: 'Most of us try to stay up as long as we can after night duty, then we sleep better that evening before the early morning watch. It seems to work better that way.'

Every session I was becoming faster and more confident, so after a week I was moved to a busier station. There were constant enemy attacks on the docks at Portsmouth and Plymouth but a lot of our work was plotting coastal command patrols. Every morning there was the *Milk Run* when Sunderland flying boats patrolled areas of the Atlantic looking out for merchant vessels needing air support. The U-boats operating from France were very active at that time and we were losing many vessels and their cargoes of essential supplies, as well as the crews. In addition, many of the fighter squadrons in our Group were called out to intercept German bombers.

We would initiate Air Sea Rescue whenever possible if any of our aircraft were shot down. One of the most satisfying nights of all was when I plotted in one of our bombers from 340 miles away as it gradually lost height. It was showing Broad IF, the Mayday signal, and finally it crashed into the English Channel. I was informed sometime later that all the crew had been picked up by Dover ASR half a mile from my last plot. I felt then that every effort I'd made in the past few weeks was worthwhile if I had helped to save that crew.

The London Blitz was still continuing and enemy bombers crossed the coast in our area on the way to their target, whilst Luftwaffe pilots returning home would frequently stray and jettison their bombs. That meant there were often dog-fights over our area. It was an exciting time. After the initial month working at Rudloe Manor I received my first promotion. Aircraftswoman 2nd Class 445020 became Aircraftswoman 1st Class, with a very small increase in my fortnightly pay.

As the weeks went by I got to know my fellow WAAF of C Watch. Working in the unusual and sometimes difficult conditions below ground ensured we worked as a team. They were an eclectic mix. There were daughters of bankers, stockbrokers and a vicar amongst us. There were two Canadian volunteers. Many of the girls, whether officers or other ranks, had family or boyfriends serving as air crew with Fighter or Bomber Command. Girls from wealthy backgrounds were mixed with bright girls from lower income families like mine. They came from all parts of the country and predominantly were educated at either grammar or private schools.

The majority were quick, both manually and mentally, and all spoke clearly. If a Plotter, Filterer, or the Duty Controller had to ask a second time for a position or information to be repeated or clarified there would be a delay. A fighter interception could be missed, an air sea rescue postponed and aircrew perish. It could mean identifying an approaching hostile too late, delaying both air raid warnings and the scrambling of our fighters. There would be more damage to docks, factories, airfields and homes, and more civilians would die or be injured. The organisation of every detail of the Radar chain seemed to have been meticulously planned and was dependent upon fast and mutual co-operation.

As well as a lot of hard work and hours spent underground, there were happy and relaxed times too. When off duty we would go to the weekly station dances where non-commissioned pilots from local airfields would be invited. Often we met Sergeant Pilots from RAF Colerne and got to know our Polish and Czech allies.

These young men were extraordinary. They had a special air of bravado about them. Far from their homeland and without news of the fate of their families, they fought every air battle with intensity. They hated the enemy bitterly and were the bravest of the brave, often risking everything to get a kill. One of the Polish pilots was notorious for flying low down the valley and then passing the Officers' Mess almost at eye level. Whenever he was chastised for this, he always said: 'Not me – that my brother Josef!'

As soon as I had a day off I visited Bath for the first time. I was touched by its beauty. The city is situated in a basin, with the houses climbing the hills that encircle the centre. It is constructed in creamy gold sandstone taken from the quarries at Corsham. I had written to my aunt and uncle to tell them I was nearby. Their house lay on the far hillside of the city. I had not seen much of Uncle Wilfred and Auntie Did since I was a child but they gave me a great welcome. They said how much they appreciated the fact that I had joined the RAF to take the place of their son Eric after he was killed.

My aunt – nicknamed Didymus as she was the survivor of a twin birth – showed me around the city. She had been a magistrate for many years and on several occasions I went with her to the law court to listen to some of the cases. She was very strict although the offences were mostly *drunk and disorderly* or minor assaults, as crime was not a great problem in Bath at the time. My uncle worked for a large industrial concern as an engineer. Their only other child, my cousin Daphne, was away on the academic staff at Leeds University, involved in research on the first computers. Whereas I had joined the forces, she after losing her brother became a confirmed pacifist.

I enjoyed my days off and being back in a family home. Both my aunt and uncle were keen musicians and they roped me in to play the piano whilst they played the cello and violin. We would attempt to play several well-known classical compositions but I am afraid, despite eight years of piano lessons, I was not a natural musician and had to painstakingly read the music each time. Obviously my efforts did not add much to the musicality of the performances. So that ordeal soon stopped. However, they were lovely people and forgave me my shortcomings in that direction.

After two months on plotting duties I was called into the office of the officer in charge of the Filter Room, Wing Commander Rudd. 'I have been watching you. You are obviously good at mathematics so I have a special task for you.'

He wanted me to design a distorted grid of the Filter Room table, as if it were part of a globe. I had a week to produce it. To this day I am not clear how this could work. It would have been far more difficult for the Filterer to correct the positions of the plots but I agreed to have a go. I was given a small office to myself and some mathematical instruments to use. It meant I worked days only and for a week I managed to have a proper night's sleep, which was a great incentive. Seven days later I handed in my effort. I never knew whether it was used.

Meanwhile I had noticed on Daily Routine Orders, posted each morning on the notice board, that there was a demand for volunteers to train as Intelligence Officers. I had previously considered applying for a commission as a Code and Cipher Officer but it did not really appeal to me. This was different. I immediately submitted an application to the Senior Admin Officer.

It was August and the weather was very hot and humid. A few days later, after a busy night watch, Ruth and I both decided to sleep on the grass in the garden in our pyjamas. Around midday, I was awakened by Mrs. Clarke who had returned home for lunch. 'You are wanted on the phone immediately. They said it's urgent.' I wondered what I had done. There was a message for me to report immediately to Wing Commander Rudd's office. Transport would be sent to pick me up in half an hour. I had not completely woken up but realised something strange was happening. I dressed and arrived at the Wingco's office in record time.

'Sit down,' he said. 'I have called you in to tell you I am putting you forward for a commission as a Filterer Officer. I think you will do well.'

Confused, I replied: 'But Sir, I have just applied for an Intelligence commission.'

'You won't get it; I'll make sure of that. We need good Filterers desperately and that is what you will be.' He was not angry but very firm. 'You can go now, and think about what I have said.' Returning to Corsham I was thinking hard. What did I want to do? Would I have any choice?

A week later, I received instructions to report to Air Ministry for the interview for an Intelligence Commission. 'So he hasn't put a stop to that,' I thought. I received permission from the duty officer to attend and was given my travel warrant. As I was going off duty, Wing Commander Rudd called me in to his office. 'It's no point in you going you know. I'll stop it.' He smiled knowingly. I still could not believe this possible and two days later, I was at Air Ministry reporting for my interview.

The officer at reception told me to go to Room 153 and wait. I went up to the first floor and found the room. I knocked, there was no reply. I knocked again, still nothing, so I opened the door. The room was empty. I sat down at the desk and waited. High up on the far wall were three small windows looking down into the room. Several people appeared and gazed down at me and then moved on. I do not recall exactly how long I waited, but it was well over an hour and a half and still nobody appeared. I realised then that the Wing Commander had succeeded and I would not be seen by anyone. Finally I got up and left. Two days later, I received instructions to go to RAF Bawdsey to train as a Filterer Officer.

When I recently applied for my WAAF records, I found marked on them: "Applied for Intelligence commission. Found not suitable." Since I was never interviewed, I wonder what really happened. Perhaps if I had reported to reception that no one had come to interview me and asked why, I might have found it was a mistake; or perhaps not. But I was young, only a humble ACW1, intimidated by the sanctity of Air Ministry and already discouraged by the Wingco's insistence he would block y application. So I just walked out of the building and returned to RAF Rudloe Manor.

The Home of Radar

In February 1937, Bawdsey Manor near the village of Bawdsey in Suffolk became the centre for research into the use of RDF (Range and Direction Finding) for military use. A team of scientists headed by Robert Watson Watt moved its operations there and became RAF Bawdsey. This was the beginning of the Radar chain of defence. The first Filter Room to process the information received from the Chain Home stations was sited here in May of the same year. This was where I was to train as a Filterer Officer.

The nearest railway station was Felixstowe. I arrived there at midday. A transport was waiting. I joined five other WAAF and we were told we would be taken to the ferry as the camp was on the other side of the Deben River. It appeared all six of us were on the same course, hoping to become officers. There were seven Filter Rooms covering the coastline of Britain and Northern Ireland and each of us had come from a different Fighter Group. On the short journey to the ferry we compared notes. We seemed to range in age from twenty to twenty-four years and have similar educational backgrounds with a bias to mathematics.

The ferry trip was a surprise. I had imagined it would be a fairly large vessel but it turned out to be a small boat taking no more than eight people, with an outboard engine. The ferryman was a RAF Corporal. It seemed the camp was fairly isolated. Each time we wished to leave we had to take the ferry. The journey had one feature I will always remember. As the boat travelled through the water it left a luminous stream in its wake. Apparently this was a characteristic of the coastal waters in that region. I wondered whether it could be seen by enemy aircraft.

As we walked towards the Manor we saw the four 350 foot transmitting towers of the CH Radar station with curtain arrays of aerials strung across them. It was impressive. The Victorian manor house too was an amazing sight with its surrounding towers and ornate series of steps leading up to the entrance. Sited on the top of the rising ground, it looked out over terraced gardens and nearby woods and the vast lawns led to the cliffs overlooking the sea. We were to learn that there was no chance of swimming from the beach, which was surrounded by barbed wire and mined. This part of the coastline was considered a possible landing area for any German invasion.

The Manor housed the station HQ, the WAAF sleeping quarters, the Other Ranks' dining Room and the Officers' Mess. The specially built Operations block was camouflaged and a short distance from the main buildings. Due to the importance of the base, there was a contingent of soldiers permanently guarding it. The Highland Light Infantry complete with their kilts were on duty as we entered.

Checking in, we were assigned our sleeping quarters. They were right at the top of the house where I imagine the servants once slept. Every room had a fantastic view out to sea. I was to share with Jean, who had been working at the Newcastle Filter Room. She was a year older than me and also a grammar school girl. The communal bathroom for our use was amazing. 'Just look at this!' Jean said. There was an enormous roll top bath and the toilet was decorated with a pink floral design. Even in the servants' quarters the bedrooms were spacious. The utility RAF furniture was lost in them. After unpacking we returned to the main hall.

We were welcomed by the Squadron Leader in charge and introduced to the Scientific Officer and the two WAAF Section Officers who were to be our instructors for the next two weeks. The course would consist of several lectures on advanced technical knowledge of Radar and the new search methods being introduced, as well as practical experience.

Most of our time would be spent in the Filter Room learning the essential techniques for using the information displayed by the Plotters and turning it into recognisable tracks of friendly and hostile aircraft for advance warning of air raids, Mayday incidents and positions of friendly aircraft. We were told it would be 'practice, practice and more practice' until we were both speedy in our actions and correct in our calculations. It was emphasised that many had failed in the past to reach the necessary standard and had been returned to their units. Our commission as officers was not assured.

We realised how important it was to succeed. In order to operate the seven Filter Rooms and allow some break from the intensive and onerous duties of a Filterer, more trained officers were needed. As we left for our evening meal we discussed the responsibilities we were being trained to assume. It was obvious we had a vital part to play in the defence of our country. As I was getting to know these other young women, I realised how in this war women were taking over important roles in defending their homeland.

On the following morning we were taken to the Chain Home Radar station operating on the site, to see how the information the Filter Plotters received was obtained. The area covered by the transmitter was an arc over the North Sea and the continent of Europe. We were shown how aircraft in this area would reflect a response from the transmitter's radio waves. It appeared as a beating echo on the linear trace of light running across the cathode ray tube. The distance covered by the transmission of radio waves was up to three hundred miles. The position of the echo received from the aircraft showed its distance from the Radar site. A goniometer was used to estimate the azimuth or angle of approach. This information could be converted into a plan position on the gridded map and relayed to the Filter Room table.

We were shown how pulse transmissions of radio waves produced a polar diagram and how every Radar station had its own individual one. Coverage was not solid but consisted of a series of lobes of energy. We had to take this into consideration in our filtering calculations. It was getting complicated. June whispered to me: 'I'll never pass, I don't understand a thing.' I said nothing. It was not going to be easy.

After four hours of trying to absorb all this new technical information we returned to the Manor, our brains full of part knowledge and part questions. Fortunately the afternoon session was a little easier. We were taken to the training Filter Room where we would learn how to use the information displayed by the plotters connected to the various Radar stations. We only spent a short time there. As we left the instructor said: 'You'll have to get down to putting what you have learned today into practice tomorrow morning. Now go and have a break.'

Thankfully we returned to the house for a meal and relaxed in the garden, discussing the day's activities. Someone said: 'Do you think we'll ever get the hang of it?' I think we were all wondering whether we would make the grade.

We were both excited and a little daunted by the task ahead of us. Nevertheless the next morning we were up early, ready to start our first day in the Filter Room. The training table was a replica of one used at 11 Group Filter Room at Fighter Command Headquarters at Stanmore in Middlesex. It was also designed to be used as a reserve centre should Stanmore be bombed. There was the customary table with the gridded map covering from Norfolk to the Isle of Wight and extending over the English Channel and part of continental Europe.

Airwomen were already sitting at their appointed stations preparing a mock series of incidents extending all over the table. The instructor took over. 'You already know from your previous work as Plotters that the number on the circular plot changes with the Sector Clock and represents the time when the information was displayed. The first thing to remember is that you only combine information from different Radar stations on what appears to be the same aircraft track, with counters containing a similar number.'

She reminded us that every station was allotted a separate colour and continued: 'On the table you will see arcs, emanating from each site at ten mile intervals, extending over the whole table. These bear the same colour as the station's plots. As soon as information on a new track appears you must put a halma down. On getting a second plot from an adjoining station, the interception of the ranges will give you your first filtered position so you can place your first directional arrow. You then call to the Raid Orderly for the next numbered track. She will hand you the metal stand bearing the next raid number.' She paused and looked to see if we had any questions.

'The two stations will continue displaying more information, indicating estimated height and number of aircraft and whether it is showing IFF. You are already familiar with this of course. The job of the Filterer is to assess the correct numbers and height, bearing in mind the position of the stations reporting. One station may have a more accurate assessment of the number of aircraft dependent upon its position in relation to the incoming or outgoing track. You must get to know all the sites and their individual polar diagrams in order to make a swift decision.' She paused. 'Don't worry, after some practice, you will be doing it automatically.' I turned and looked at Jean. I'm sure she was feeling as doubtful as I was.

In turn we filtered our first estimated position and then as more plots appeared we put down the first arrow giving the up-to-date position and the direction. We then had to calculate the number of aircraft. Was it 10+ or 30+? Which information was more reliable? One station gave the height as 15,000 feet, using only the figure 15, the other estimated 20. The decision was in our hands. As the morning proceeded, most of us seemed to be getting it right. But we were very slow. It was a thrill the first time I heard the teller passing on my filtered information: 'Standby, Hostile two four zero, south west Willie Victor five three, six zero, fifteen plus at twenty.'

As each new track started, it would be identified by the Controller on the balcony above the table, based on his previous knowledge of movements of all friendly aircraft. If it was not one of ours it was theirs, a hostile – *reductio ad absurdum*. The only exceptions would occur when a pilot omitted to turn on his identification signal IFF. Sometimes this was intentional, as many pilots believed that German Radar could pick them up. We were assured this was not the case but I could understand a pilot's reluctance. Other instances would occur during the return of our bombers after a raid. A damaged bomber might lose his IFF signal and be too damaged to keep up with the mainstream. These stragglers might return off course. We were told to recognise this possibility.

The first day's practice ended. It had been a lot to absorb. Six very tired WAAF sat down and compared notes. Jean said she had enjoyed it. I had too but Sylvia, a plotter from 13 Group Inverness, seemed worried. 'This is not for me, I can't keep up. I'm going to ask to see the Squadron Leader and tell him.'

We tried to reassure her, pointing out that it was only the first day. She agreed reluctantly to wait a further day to see how it went. Jean spoke to me quietly: 'She's not going to make it; she was shaking like an aspen leaf as she was filtering.'

On the second day, after a morning and afternoon session, I felt more confident in what I had to do. The instructor was watching me and then she said: 'You're ambidextrous aren't you?' I nodded. 'That will help you!'

By the end of the day, we had all speeded up, except for Sylvia. 'I can't go on,' she said and burst into tears. She ran out of the room and by the time we returned to the Manor she was packing. The Squadron Leader had arranged for her to return to Inverness. I realised that as well as skill and speed we would need to find an inner strength if we wanted to become successful Filterers. There would be intense pressure in times of heavy activity.

And so it continued – at least one and sometimes two sessions in the Filter Room, practising every day, getting more confidence and working faster. There were several more technical lectures, sometimes in the evening. Even these became easier to understand.

I realised what an incredible system had been built on Watson Watt's original experiments. The linking together of the chain of Radar stations, the Filter Rooms and the Operations Rooms had created a formidable defence barrier around our coasts. After the war, it was suggested that German Radar was more advanced than ours. That may have been true – but the way they used it could never compare with our Chain Home system. Their units worked independently of each other whereas British Radar was linked as a defence chain around the British Isles.

There was not much free time for entertainment. At the end of a long day, we had neither sufficient energy nor inclination to go out. We would wander around the beautiful grounds and walk over to the edge of the cliffs and gaze at the sea, but mostly it was early bed for us all.

At the end of the first week we managed a trip into Felixstowe via the ferry boat. We saw a film and called in the Services Club for a meal. We arrived back at Bawdsey Manor in time to spend a couple of hours dancing with the Highland Light Infantry at the base camp. But really we were pretty exhausted; the course was demanding and the hours long. Sunday came and went with a compulsory church parade, a quiet amble round the grounds and a phone call home. No news of George.

The second week was spent once more practising on the table every day for hours. We had just one more lecture explaining how our filtered information, told to the Operations Room, was used to give air raid warnings, initiate interception of hostiles, passed on to coastal gun crews for gun-laying, and above all used by Air Sea Rescue to pick up ditched aircrews, whether friendly or hostile.

Friday was our final day. We completed a written test and had one final practical filtering session, prior to hearing whether we had passed the course. During the afternoon, we were called into the Squadron Leader's office to hear our results. All five of us had passed.

We were handed our white Officer Cadet bands to put around our hats and given our travel warrants to proceed to the Officer Cadet Training Unit (OCTU) at Loughborough College. Finally we were told where we would be posted, assuming we passed our Officers course. It was explained that we would be sent to the quieter groups first to gain more experience. These would be Inverness, Northern Ireland or Preston. As we became more proficient, we would be moved to busier Filter Rooms. I waited to hear my posting.

'Cadet Officer Le Croissette, you will be reporting to 9 Group, RAF Barton Hall, Preston.' 'I've never been to Lancashire – they say the people are very friendly there,' I said to myself. 'Thank you, Sir,' and I saluted. 'Good luck, you've done well.' That evening I wrote to George telling him the news.

I was going to be an officer!

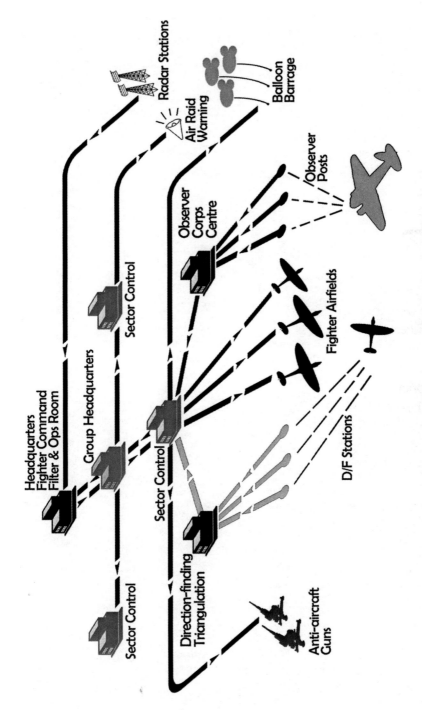

Radar Stations

Balloon Barrage

Air Raid Warning

Observer Posts

Observer Corps Centre

Sector Control

Group Headquarters

Headquarters Fighter Command Filter & Ops Room

Sector Control

Fighter Airfields

D/F Stations

Sector Control

Direction-finding Triangulation

Anti-aircraft Guns

Diagram showing how the Filter Room was central to Britain's air defence

Francois, Jean and Hélène

No.2 WAAF Officers' Mess, Bentley Manor after the fire

Overview of 11 Group Filter Room, Fighter Command HQ

Details of the Filter Room Table, Fighter Command HQ

Peter's semi-pro Big Band

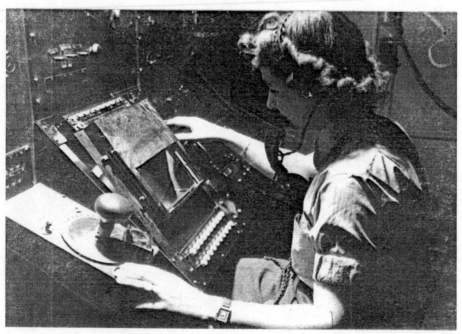

South Coast Radar Operator at her Cathode Ray tube

The grim entrance to Breendonk Concentration Camp

Flight Officer Grogono - (Grog)

Launch of a V2 rocket

Our wedding present from cartoonist Bill Hooper (Raff)

Receiving the King's Commission

RAF Loughborough was housed in the college there and had only been used since July 1941 as the WAAF Officer Cadet Training Unit. Prior to that date, women officers in the RAF did not hold the King's Commission although they often had men serving under them. We were one of the earliest intakes to have this honour.

Together with the other four Filterers, I arrived there in late August 1941. This made us one of the first groups to swear allegiance to our monarch. During our journey together from Felixstowe we discussed our apprehensions about what we would have to do on the commissioning course. None of us had any idea of what we would have to face. We were mostly grammar school girls from a middle-class background and quite young to take on great responsibilities.

We did not realise that instructions had been given that we were not to be failed on the Cadet course, except under the most extreme circumstances, such as a grave act of misbehaviour or complete stupidity. As we had already passed the technical test as Filterers, which was rated as Top Secret, it was vital we passed. We had already signed the Official Secrets Act, which forbade us discussing our work for thirty years. Furthermore, we were required to replace the men currently working in the Filter Rooms who were needed overseas.

The commissioning course lasted for a week and was very intensive. During our stay we would have to prove we were capable of taking command of both airwomen and airmen. We would have to learn how to lead official marching ceremonies, take the salute, carry out kit inspections and put delinquent personnel on a charge. We would learn about the history of the Royal Air Force, what King's Regulations (KRs) were and how to comport ourselves in the Officers' Mess. We would find out what items in the Mess we had to pay for and the duties of the President of the Messing Committee (PMC).

After the briefing we were allocated rooms in the student quarters. They were sparsely furnished but adequate. There was a desk and chair together with a notebook provided for making notes during the lectures. There was a special dining Mess for us to use where we would get used to Officers' Mess procedures. The first evening we had our initial lecture on the duties of an officer. From then onwards the days were full with lectures, drills and tests. My mind was filled with RAF jargon – AWOL, absent without leave; DRO, daily routine orders. My legs ached with marching and my right arm with saluting. The evenings were spent acclimatising ourselves to the Mess procedures.

It was pointed out that in some stations we would share a Mess with the male officers and they had a lot of tradition we would have to learn. I had never drunk any alcohol up to that time and wondered how I would get on when there was the toast to His Majesty! All the time I felt we were being observed. I guessed it was to see if we were capable of behaving *as an officer and a gentleman!* But the other girls seemed just as overwhelmed with the Officers' Mess experience as I was – all except Cynthia who was the only one whose background had accustomed her to service life as her father was a Colonel.

Above all we were anxious about passing the final test. There was no time for any frivolity. We stayed together and exchanged notes each evening. 'Do you think we'll have to remember all that history about the Flying Corps?' asked Maggie, the oldest one amongst us.

On the last morning all five of us were told we had passed the course and had been judged fit to receive the King's Commission. We then had to swear our loyalty to King George VI. The rest of the intake would have to do their specific training courses before they became officers. It was only then that I realised how different our life would be from theirs.

The remainder were due to become either code and cipher or admin officers. Thank goodness I was not one of them. They would have to carry out the everyday duties of running the units, organising kit inspections, supervising the airwomen's well-being and coping with their misdemeanours; possibly dealing with the ones who became pregnant. Because our duties were carried out both during the day and the night and our sleep patterns were changing constantly, we never had to attend any parades, inspections or church services. I realised that someone had to carry out these supervisory duties but I was glad that I was going to do something that might help to win the war.

After having been confirmed in the rank of Assistant Section Officer – equivalent to a Pilot Officer – we were instructed to choose a tailor to make our uniform. This consisted of two tunics, two skirts, two shirts, a tie, a hat and a greatcoat. We were granted the sum of £50 to cover this but in the future we would be responsible for buying any replacements or additional items we needed.

Details were taken of our bank accounts since our monthly pay would be paid direct. We were to receive £10 a month and from that we would have to pay our Mess bills. I realised I would have to wait over four weeks before it would arrive, so I carefully guarded my final pay as an airwoman to see me through. We were then told we would have a week's leave, during which time we had to get our uniforms made, ready to report to our new units in eight days time. Many of the girls received an allowance from home but I had to manage on my service pay.

I said goodbye to the four new WAAF Filterer officers who had been with me for the last three weeks. Since we would all be working in Filter Rooms, we guessed we would one day meet up again somewhere, or at least make contact through the telephone lines between stations. Taking the next train to London, I arrived home unexpectedly. My parents were delighted to see me and I think quite proud of their Assistant Section Officer daughter. First thing next day I was walking up and down Savile Row in the centre of London's tailoring district, deciding whom I would patronise. Hector Powe got my vote, I have no idea why.

Entering the shop I was greeted by an assistant who, seeing the white cadet band round my hat, asked: 'Are you here to order your uniform?' From then on it was tape measuring every part of me with figures marked carefully in a book. The whole process took about forty minutes. 'Right,' he said. 'It will be ready in three days time for a fitting.'

'I'm due to report to my new station on Sunday.'

'Don't worry, it will be ready and we will deliver it to your home in time.' And so it was, the fitting was perfect and two days later everything arrived in a smart Hector Powe box. The whole lot cost me 47 pounds, 15 shillings and sixpence. I had enough left to buy two extra shirts and two Van Heusen collars that did not have to be starched!

The next morning I was due to get the ten o'clock train to Preston. I had a lot to do. I would have plenty of luggage to carry; my kitbag with all my airwoman's uniform in it to be returned to stores, as well as a new suitcase full of what I needed for my life as an officer. It was a beautiful autumn morning as I set off for my journey to RAF Barton Hall. I was feeling extremely warm as I had to wear my new greatcoat. There was no room to pack it. So complete with kitbag, suitcase and gas mask I set off for my next challenge. As I walked down the street to the bus stop, an airman passed me, turned his head towards me and saluted. I was so surprised I almost forgot to salute back. 'Something else I've got to get used to,' I thought to myself.

First Tracks

I had never travelled First Class on a train before, but when I arrived at Euston station and showed my travel warrant to the porter he helped me carry my luggage to a first class compartment and put it on the rack for me. It took me a few moments to realise he was waiting for a tip. I gave him a shilling, having no idea how much he was expecting. I had never tipped anyone before so this was another new experience.

The compartment was empty except for an elderly, or so it appeared to me, Army Colonel and one civilian. The Colonel gave me a cursory glance and went back to his paper. I got the feeling he didn't approve of women officers. I sat on the opposite seat and took out a book.

The journey would last more than two hours, so I had brought some corned beef sandwiches with me but I wondered if I dared eat them. Would the Colonel disapprove? I was not sure how officers behaved in such circumstances, since there was no restaurant car. Everything seemed a learning process to me at that time. Fortunately he got out at Birmingham and the carriage filled with some RAF types, so I ate my sandwiches and chatted with them.

Arriving at Preston, there was a RAF transport picking up the air crew and they offered to drop me off en route at the entrance to Barton Hall. It was located quite a way out in the country between the villages of Broughton and Barton. It seemed that most Filter Rooms were sited in remote locations, no doubt for security reasons. Checking in, I was shown my quarters on the main site. It was rather more commodious than my airwoman's accommodation and, of course, no horrible *biscuits* to sleep on. I had my first meal in the Officers' Mess. There I learnt I would be joining A watch and I was due on duty at midnight.

It was already early evening, so that after unpacking my belongings it was time to take the transport to the Filter Room. Three other WAAF Officers joined me and introduced themselves. The leader of the watch was older than I and had joined the WAAF at the outbreak of war. Her name was Mary Bear and she did her best to help me during my first experience of real life operations. She acted like a mother hen to us all. Her first words to me were: 'If you have any problems, just come and find me, any time of day or night.'

The site was a short distance from the main house in Langley Lane. The complex known as 9 Group Operations Centre consisted of three separate bunkers a few hundred yards from each other. One was used as the Operations Room; the second was the Filter Room and the third the Communications Centre. These bunkers were built on the same principle as those at 12 Group Watnall and 13 Group Inverness. The buildings were partially buried and then made into hillocks, a huge amount of grassed soil covering them for protection.

As I entered the Filter Room I could see that it followed a similar pattern to the one I had used during training – a large gridded table covering the coastline from north Wales up to the west coast of Scotland, with the balcony above housing the Movements Liaison Section, Filter Officer and Controller, with the Tellers and Speed Orderly in their own corner. My first night went by peaceably with very little activity. It gave me a chance to learn the names of the Radar stations feeding us with information and to get to know the rest of the watch, three other young women.

During the following days I found there was considerably less activity than at 10 Group. Consequently the nights were often long and boring and the bunker was quite cold. We would wear everything we could find to keep warm. Many of the personnel took books with them or did sewing or knitting to keep themselves occupied on the long night watches. It was also an opportunity for the plotters to bind with Radar operators on the other end of their telephone line.

At the outset I wondered how I would cope, giving orders instead of taking them, but I found it came naturally. I had never suffered from lack of confidence and having been a plotter I knew exactly what needed to be done and done swiftly. I found no difficulty in giving vital instructions when necessary. Every Filterer Officer appointed had always started as a Plotter and it was obvious this was essential in order to understand where mistakes might occur. Of course, I too took orders from the Controller and the Duty Filter Officer. This was the chain of command. We had very little communication with other parts of the Group Headquarters since all Special Duties personnel lived a somewhat isolated existence from the rest of the camp.

I do remember that initially I retained a fear of the admin WAAF Flight Sergeant, barely restraining myself from saluting her before she saluted me! Flight Sergeant Brimblecombe was a terror and bullied the airwomen continuously. If their hair was too long – it should never touch the collar of one's jacket – she would put the poor unfortunate airwoman on a charge. She made no exceptions if anyone broke the rules.

In the first few days the Controllers also intimidated me somewhat. They were men in their mid-forties and pre-war had responsible posts in either the Stock Exchange or banking, but after a while, as I got to know them, I found most of them both friendly and helpful. Knowing that there was a good deal more responsibility now on my shoulders and that we were often dealing with life and death situations increased my sense of dedication and duty.

There were occasional bombing raids on the docks in Liverpool and the war factories around Manchester. The majority of the tracks we filtered were student pilots on training flights or Coastal Command patrols over the Irish Sea and the Pacific. On several occasions, we encountered official flights, returning dignitaries from conferences in the United States just prior to and after they entered the war at the year end.

On one unforgettable occasion a particular flight approaching from Ireland showed no IFF identification and did not relate to any known movement, so it was identified as an X or doubtful raid. About fifty miles from the coast it was finally recognised as friendly. It was Winston Churchill returning earlier than scheduled from a conference with President Roosevelt. The pilot had forgotten to turn on his IFF signal! Fortunately, as no enemy aircraft normally would attack from that direction, no fighters were sent out to intercept it. I wonder if Churchill ever knew he had come in as an unidentified aircraft

Although this posting gave me practice and confidence in filtering, it was not one I particularly enjoyed. There was little to do off the base. Preston was neither a particularly pleasant town nor a welcoming one. I had always believed the Lancashire people to be friendly but at that time they made no contact with us. On the contrary, if we went into town they would brush past us. Mothers with prams would almost run us down. If they had realised the conditions we were working under and the hours we were on duty, perhaps they would have had more respect for us. Furthermore, since most of the men working in the Filter Room were considerably older than us, they offered little temptation compared to aircrew.

The Officers' Mess was quite small and provided little in-camp entertainment. We were thrown on to our own resources. Because of a shortage of personnel, we were working a three-watch basis, which meant there was little spare time between watches after sleeping, eating and carrying out any necessary domestic duties. However, I made friends with a Canadian Section Officer, Collette Duval, who worked in the Ops Room. She was a well-known cellist and prior to joining up was playing in the orchestra of the Sadler's Wells Ballet.

When the company came on tour to a Manchester theatre I accompanied her and met many of the dancers and members of the orchestra. Collette was also a spiritualist and persuaded me to go to one of the services. They sang a few hymns, not the usual ones heard in a church but rather more surreal. Then the speaker, a well-known medium, gave her address. It was almost a séance as she would pick on people in the congregation and give them a message from those *who had passed over*. She suddenly pointed to me and insisted I had a great aura around me but there was no interesting message. I was not convinced.

An interesting incident happened during one of our night watches. Squadron Leader Daniel Meinertzhagen, who came from a well-known and extremely rich banking family, was the Controller for that night. During the watch, news came through that a team of Special Operations soldiers had landed at Radio Fecamp, the famous pre-war off-shore radio station. It had been taken over by the German army and was being used to transmit radio signals, guiding bombing raids to their target.

The British force succeeded in capturing an important German scientist who was carrying out special experiments on new equipment there. He was brought back for questioning. During the raid much of the station was destroyed. On learning this, Daniel Meinertzhagen was most indignant. 'How dare they!' he shouted, 'They never asked my father's permission!' He was not one of my favourite officers. He never mixed with the rest of us like most of the other senior officers. I found him rather arrogant.

Christmas arrived and there was an effort to provide some entertainment for the personnel. The airwomen had several dances arranged for them. Our watch was on duty throughout the night of Christmas Eve. Since it was the custom for the officers to serve the celebration lunch to the other ranks on Christmas Day, this meant we had a very brief sleep before we reported to their Mess for the occasion. Despite our tiredness, we enjoyed serving them as we realised how hard our Plotters worked. Only very recently I had a phone call from one of the Plotters who had been at the Christmas meal and had read my recent autobiography. She had kept a copy of the menu and she sent it on to me. Memories came flooding back as I read the signatures of those people present at that meal and with whom I had spent so many working hours in the dark days of war.

This is how their menu read:

Christmas Menu

Soup

Cream of Tomato

Joints and Poultry

Roast Pork   Roast Turkey and Chicken
Apple Sauce   Chestnut Stuffing
Brussels Sprouts   Cauliflower

Sweets

Christmas Pudding and White Sauce
Mince Pies
Dessert Cigarettes
Beer and Minerals

****

I imagine it was a good deal more than civilians could have managed on their rations.

The winter of 1941/42 was extremely cold and coming off duty at midnight in snow and ice we often waited outside the bunker for transport for up to a half hour. This resulted in many airwomen going down with colds and other infections. Having always suffered from bronchial catarrh, I wasn't at all surprised to succumb to a bout of it. I would cough my way through the eight-hour watch but there was no chance of going off sick as I did not have a temperature. To add to the gloom, a couple of weeks later I contracted chicken pox. Never having had it as a child, I was really spotty! I had eighty-six eruptions on my face alone. No-one could come and visit me in the sick bay unless they had already had it, so I spent two miserable weeks in a room on my own.

On my return to duty, there was one bright spot. The senior Royal Observer Corps officer invited me out to dinner. He had his own car and a large private income. We went to the famous Moorcock Inn, high in the hills at Clitheroe. It was a memorable night as for the first time I drank alcohol.

Many years before I had signed the pledge, vowing that alcohol would never pass my lips. Having been brought up as a Baptist, I was prevailed upon to sign this when quite young, probably fourteen years of age. This particular evening I decided it was time at last to try the evil drink. My escort knew his way around the menu and I left it to him to choose the meal. This was my first experience of a high-class restaurant, a few meals at a Lyons Corner House being the height of my previous gastronomic experience.

We started with a Rye Highball with the first course, a consommé. The main dish of locally reared venison was accompanied by a bottle of vintage Burgundy, and after a chocolate dessert and then cheese we finished with a Van der Hum liqueur. There was little sign of rationing at this hotel, high in the Waddington Fell near the source of the River Ribble, and the meal was delicious.

I soon realised I must have a strong head for liquor because I returned to report for duty at midnight and worked safely until 0800 hours the following morning. My companion was about forty years old and married. He spent the whole meal talking about his wife and little boy. He showed me their photos. I could see he was missing them. I hope my companion enjoyed my conversation, since that was all he got out of it.

It was during my time at Barton Hall that we saw the success of new technology to counteract German navigational and bombing aids. It was codenamed Operation Aspirin. The German scientists had perfected the *Knickenbein*, a radio navigational aid to improve their bombing technique. Radio beams were sent out from two different stations and the point where they crossed indicated the target for the night's operation. They were having considerable success with this method. Our boffins got to work to counteract this and perfected a system to intercept and interfere with the direction of the beams, thus diverting the target area. Our counter device was named Operation Aspirin! The process was known to us as *bending the beam*.

During one eventful evening duty, we received news from a secret source that Liverpool was that night's target. It was many years later that I realised this information was coming from Bletchley Park through Enigma intercepts. Aspirin was to be used in our area for the first time and the boffins successfully manipulated the point where the beams intersected to an alternative site – Dublin! It gave us great satisfaction in the Filter Room that night as the bomber raid headed in the wrong direction. We were aware that the neutral Irish Republic especially Dublin, was used to harbour German spies attempting to infiltrate into Britain through our western coastline.

I was to stay at 9 Group until the spring of 1942. By early March I was considered a competent Filterer and I was promoted to Section Officer. Instead of a narrow ring round the sleeve of my uniform, I now had a wider one. This was equivalent to Flying Officer in the RAF or First Lieutenant in the Army. Even better was the news that I was being posted back to 10 Group, Rudloe Manor. That night I celebrated.

Back to Bath

It was like coming home. I arrived back at Rudloe Manor, this time as an officer. No more being billeted out or relying upon transport to get on duty, instead I had a pleasant room to myself on the main camp and shared a batwoman with two other officers – no more bed-making. It was no distance to the Manor where all the admin offices were, as well as the Officers' Mess. This time these facilities were for both WAAF and RAF officers. I immediately found a very friendly atmosphere and I already knew many of the WAAF officers from my time there as a Plotter. They gave me a great welcome.

The most senior was Flight Officer Sadie Younger, a member of the Scottish brewing family. She had taken on the job of providing flowers for the dining tables and, despite having little facilities or money, managed with great ingenuity to provide elaborate and sometimes unusual decorations. On one particular occasion she produced a huge bowl of golden flowers for the top table and assured us none of the senior officers would recognise them. She had used dandelions, or as the French call them *pissenlit,* and had made a great mass of their bright yellow flower heads to create the effect. Needless to say, no-one recognised their floral centrepiece as the much despised weed and the gold braid thought they looked magnificent!

Within a very short time I adjusted to my new surroundings. Once more I was working underground in the quarries. The work here was far more interesting than 9 Group at Preston. We were still experiencing incoming German bombing raids, although by now fewer. They were mostly on docks and factories. Coastal Command however was very active over the sea around the Bay of Biscay on anti-U-boat patrols. I was excited to be told I was to visit one of their squadrons.

Although I was part of the Air Force, I had so far kept my feet firmly on the ground. But now came my first opportunity to fly. I was excited but a little nervous, especially since the plane I was to fly in was nicknamed by pilots the *Flying Coffin*. Unlike the Spitfire, Mosquito and Lancaster – all names familiar to this day – the Armstrong Whitworth Albemarle was a dud. Built as a bomber, it was no match for the Wellington and many were shot down. Its cramped fuselage meant it was little better as a transport aircraft, though it did eventually prove useful as a tug for gliders.

My Albemarle had been relegated to a reconnaissance role with Coastal Command. Apart from its reputation, this conversion gave it one rather alarming feature. The bottom of the fuselage had been replaced with clear perspex, and the observer had to lie on this to look out for U-boats in the sea below.

On this occasion, that observer was me. I certainly had a good view but it was a strange sensation, lying there with only a thin sheet of plastic beneath me and the ocean. Despite the excitement of that first flight, I was very glad when we landed safely.

By now Bomber Command was taking on a more offensive role. Many of these squadrons were based in the Midlands and north of Britain since these aircraft carried greater fuel reserves than fighters. The squadrons would join up for mass raids and we would pick them up as they crossed the coastline of 10 Group, from the Isle of Wight to north Wales.

All this, coupled with the fighter operations by squadrons based in the south-west escorting the bombers, ensured there was plenty of work to keep us busy. We much preferred this volume of activity, since the eight-hour watch would pass in a flash. The only quiet days were when the weather conditions prevented flying.

In 1939 the Admiralty had taken over a number of buildings in Bath, including the Empire Hotel, and had moved various departments there. Bath was only a few miles up the A4 from the camp. Daily there would be official cars commuting backwards and forwards to Whitehall. There was an arrangement with the RAF that if there was a spare seat, any of the officers were able to take advantage of this for a lift to visit London. On several occasions I was able to manage a short visit home on a day off between duties.

When off duty, there was always something going on in the Officers' Mess. Many fighter pilots would be sent to us for a break after completing an exhausting operational tour. They would work in the Operations Room or Communications Centre as a respite from flying. We would see them for a few weeks and then they would go back to operations. During my time at Rudloe, I met the famous "Cats Eyes" Cunningham, by then a Squadron Leader and already a successful night fighter thanks to his use of AI (Air Interception).

Another Spitfire pilot who stayed with us for a time was Mortimer Rose. He was usually the leader of any spectacular activity that these exuberant young pilots would get up to. Most of them were dare-devils and one of their favourite games was to challenge anyone who was brave enough to take a running jump from about twenty yards away and dive through the hatch of the bar. Those who failed bought drinks all round, despite any knocks or bruises they may have sustained.

There seemed to be quite a considerable connection with the stage amongst the personnel. Section Officer Janet Asherson, one of the Movements Liaison team, was the sister of Renée Asherson who started her stage career as a Shakespearian actress and went on to appear in many films. She was the wife of Robert Donat. Janet was very popular with the visiting pilots; she was tiny, extremely slim and very naive. She believed everything they told her, they teased her unmercifully!

One day they decided to fold her in half and sit her in a large waste paper basket. She fitted perfectly. She took it in good humour but insisted they buy her drinks for the rest of the evening. These young men coming off ops needed to let off steam and were capable of doing anything unexpected, but we loved them all.

Meals in a mixed Mess were formal and treated seriously. We had to be on our best behaviour and even the pilots toed the line at mealtimes. The top table with seven imposing chairs faced the rest of the room. This was where all the most senior RAF officers sat with Air Vice Marshal Orlebar, the officer commanding, in the centre.

Augustus Orlebar was one to be respected. He came from an old Bedford family and had an amazing military record. Born in 1897, he was commissioned in the Bedford Regiment in World War One and served at Gallipoli where he was wounded. He transferred to the Royal Flying Corps in 1916 and trained as a pilot. He was credited with seven kills. He served as a test pilot with the Aeronautical and Armament Experimental Establishment between the wars and was awarded the Air Force Cross and Bar. He had a career in air racing and was Officer Commanding and pilot with the High Speed Flight, the RAF's team for the Schneider Trophy, which they won in 1926 and on two further occasions Thus Britain was awarded the trophy in perpetuity. In 1929 he set an air speed record of 357.7 mph in Supermarine S.6 N247. We were all in awe of him, yet he was a most unassuming man.

It was at Rudloe that I first met Kenneth Horne, then a Squadron Leader. He was married at that time to one of our Filterers, Jo Horne, and often visited her. At the same time as being an officer in the RAF, he continued as chairman of Triplex Glass and also Chad Valley Toys. Whilst helping with the entertainment section I also met Hamilton Kennedy, an American entertainer and scriptwriter whose brother was associated with the song *You Are My Sunshine, My Only Sunshine*, so popular at the time. He was another of the ships in the night that I would have a few dinner dates with in the famous Hole in the Wall restaurant in Bath.

It was here I met and worked with Rex Harrison, who was a Captain in the Signals Corps and served as an Air Raid Warnings Officer in the Operations Room. Frequently we would be on the same night watch and he would join us for breakfast when we came off duty. He made little effort to mix with us but made sure we knew how important he was. I particularly disliked him because of his table manners. He would fill his mouth with toast and marmalade and eat so messily that the soggy bread would ooze out of the side of his mouth. Quite revolting!

At this time, although married to Colette Jackson, he was chasing after Lilli Palmer who became his second wife the following year. There was only one telephone in the Mess, situated in the anteroom. He would take it over for an hour each evening, flirting with her. Since it was in the vicinity of where many of us were relaxing, we were a reluctant party to his amorous conversations.

As much entertainment for the airwomen was organised as could be fitted in. As well as dances when soldiers from nearby barracks would be invited, we were fortunate to have Peter Hoare amongst the personnel in the PTI and Entertainments Section. He was an up and coming theatre producer before the war. He decided to produce a play and chose the comedy *French without Tears*, in which Rex Harrison had appeared pre-war.

Peter appealed for volunteers. I had always been interested in acting at school so I offered my services and was rewarded with a minor role as the French maid. I had about twenty words to say! Rex Harrison appeared at one rehearsal. Needless to say, he did not offer us any help – but we put the production on for three successive nights and the airmen and airwomen seemed to enjoy it.

As Christmas approached, our watch thought it would be a good idea to produce a pantomime. We decided on Aladdin. I was given the job of writing the parts in rhyme, or was it doggerel! I enrolled the help of my cousin and we finally came up with a script. I no longer have a copy and can only remember one phrase – *Orlebar a few* – a pun on the Air Vice Marshal's name. It was great fun doing it and all the watch became involved. It was essential to introduce some light-hearted time into the demanding days and nights of work in the Filter Room.

Air Chief Marshal Arthur Harris had taken over control of Bomber Command in February 1942. Having seen the success the Luftwaffe had in Coventry, using both bombs and incendiaries, he was planning new strategies. He decided that a city of a moderate size with some military installations would be a better target for bombing with the likelihood of greater success than a much larger industrial city spread over a wider area. He chose the city of Lubeck for the initial raid.

This medium-sized city had a port and submarine building yards nearby. The old quarters consisted mostly of timbered medieval buildings. This was the target chosen for the night of March 28th/29th, 1942. A force of 234 bombers took part. Reports came back that Lubeck went up in flames. One thousand people died and there was massive destruction. We lost 5.5% of the attacking force, no more than expected on a clear moonlit night, and the raid was hailed as a success. Hitler was incensed and ordered a series of reprisal raids against historic British towns. On the following day, Baron Gustav von Sturm, a German propagandist, is reported to have said: 'We shall go out and bomb every building in Britain marked with three stars in the Baedeker Tourist Guide.'

On the evening of April 23rd the series of Baedeker Raids began. We plotted a heavy enemy force crossing the south coast. Exeter was the first target. It was bombed for two consecutive nights. The city received considerable damage and many lives were lost. On the night of the 25th it was Bath's turn. I was on duty that night from 1600 hours to midnight. The first two hours the table was empty. We thought we were in for a quiet watch. We sat and waited, some read books, some talked. The Plotters were binding to their Radar operators. Then everything changed.

Hostile aircraft were once again reported crossing our south coast. Our fighters went out to meet them. It was not to be Exeter this time. It looked as if they were heading in our direction. Down in the quarry we could hear nothing; we relied on reports from the Royal Observer Corps. People above ground in the main camp heard and saw the bombers overhead. The continuous dull thump of the bombs as they dropped on Bath was terrifying. The old Georgian city was being pounded. The incendiaries were doing their job. Several bombs missed their target and dropped near the camp but caused no damage.

As the watch finished we came up into the fresh air just after midnight. We could see the glow as the city burned. I was worried about my aunt and uncle. They lived in Oldfield Park, only a short distance from the city centre. Early the next morning I tried to phone but all the lines were down and I was unable to leave camp. Back on duty the following night it was the same story. Bath was once more the target. First thing the following morning, I finally managed to get away to find out what had happened.

As I got off the bus in the centre of Bath I was horrified. The Assembly Building was very badly damaged. Many areas of housing were destroyed. Walking up the hill to Oldfield Park I prayed my aunt and uncle were safe. As I turned into their road I could see many houses were badly damaged; roofs missing, windows gone, walls collapsed.

Arriving at number 31, it was obvious there was blast damage; no glass in the windows and a hole in the roof but not quite as bad as I had imagined. I rang the doorbell and was relieved when my aunt opened the door. She told me they had been in the shelter and were very afraid as bombs rained down and seemed to land close by. On the first night, when it went quiet and the all clear sounded, they returned to the house. They found it had sustained a little damage but not too much.

The second night was worse. A bomb dropped very near. They could feel the vibration in the shelter and in the morning they could see how much damage the blast had caused. An incendiary had dropped through their roof. The Fire Service was soon on the scene but fortunately it was a dud and had just fizzled out without causing too much harm. They both looked very pale and shocked but seemed to be coping and had already made arrangements for essential repairs to be done. My uncle was an engineer and knew what to do. They were both in their mid-sixties but strong people. My aunt insisted 'There are many much worse off than us.'

As a Justice of the Peace, she was back on duty the following days in the magistrates' court. I was relieved they were safe but sad to see the damage done to my lovely Bath.

It was only when I arrived back at camp that I learnt that three of our Plotters had been killed. They were in Bath with their husbands and boyfriend on a short break. The hotel where they were staying had suffered a direct hit. This was a terrible blow to all of the Filter Room personnel. They were part of our team. One of the Controllers had to tell their next of kin. This was something he had not been trained to do and he was very upset when he came on duty the following night. The whole of the watch personnel felt distressed and it was hard for us to concentrate.

Bath was number two on the Baedeker list. On the 27th and 29th it was the turn of Norwich and on the 28th, York. Then the raids stopped. Had the Luftwaffe lost too many aircraft? Nothing happened for a while until Bomber Command targeted Cologne a few weeks later. Once more Baedeker was consulted and Canterbury was bombed on May 3rd and again on June 2nd and 6th. During all these Baedeker raids 1,637 people were killed and even more injured. Fifty thousand buildings were destroyed, including York's Guildhall.

Amazingly, none of the cathedrals in Norwich, Exeter or Canterbury was hit. During these raids Hitler's bombers had suffered heavy losses without causing any military damage to us. After this, bombing became sporadic, confined mostly to hit and run raids on coastal targets. The Axis needed reinforcements for the North Africa campaign and the Russian second front. Britain was to be less of a target but that did not mean we had nothing to do. Bomber Command was becoming more and more active and we plotted and filtered many outgoing mass raids, often encountering large numbers of intercepting German fighters.

It was a very stressful time as we plotted out squadron after squadron of our bombers. Many of the personnel were engaged or married to members of the crews or had relatives in Bomber Command. We always knew which squadrons were on a mission. It was amazing to watch how these girls continued to work conscientiously, even though we might track out 500 bomber aircraft and at first only 450 might return, followed much later by a few stragglers. They would never know as they continued with their plotting whether their loved ones might be amongst the missing. But they never let us down. My admiration grew more each day for these young women.

I had now been put in charge of A watch. This meant more responsibilities, as I would have to train any new Plotters and also report any airman or airwoman who was not able to cope or had personal problems, as well as ensuring I did my own work correctly. Obviously my filtering skills must have improved. One morning a few months later I was called into the office of my old friend Wing Commander Rudd. 'Eileen,' he said, 'you've done well here. We've just been asked to send a replacement Filterer Officer to Fighter Command HQ. I'm recommending you. How do you feel about that?'

'Delighted,' I replied, 'although I have loved working here.'

'Right, take a week's leave, then report to 11 Group, Stanmore.' It was early June 1943.

The Hub

I had no idea when I reported to Bentley Priory, Stanmore, Fighter Command Headquarters, how my life would change. I knew that 11 Group Filter Room was based at this key command station rather than at Group Headquarters in Uxbridge, because it covered the defence of the vital coastline from Norfolk to the Isle of Wight and of course London.

I realised that more air activity occurred in that region than anywhere else but I did not then know that Air Chief Marshal Dowding had his office there and did all his planning from that room, nor did I realise that Prime Minister Winston Churchill was a frequent visitor. I was to see both these revered personages on occasions – but only from a distance.

This was the Filter Room that had handled most of the Battle of Britain raids and the Blitz. It was the linchpin in the defence of London, where the first signs of an enemy invasion might be detected. Many of the airwomen and officers I would meet there were volunteers from the day war started. They had been chosen because they were young, quick-witted and bright. There was no time to train them in those early days, they learnt *on the job*.

One of the first officers I met was Flight Officer Grogono, known to all as Grog. She was a few years older than I was and had joined up in those early days. She was issued with a beret, an armband with WAAF on it and a raincoat. She wore her own clothes for several weeks before the uniforms arrived. Starting as a Plotter, she was moved to teller and promoted to corporal within a few weeks. She did almost every job there was in the Filter Room except Controller, which was confined to male officers. She was one of the first commissioned Special Duties WAAF and soon was working on the balcony as a Filter Officer.

I am still in touch with her. She is now ninety-three years of age and suffering from Dry Macular Degeneration, so has lost almost all of her eyesight but her spirit is indomitable. Her memory is excellent; she can still recall the names of all the Radar stations on the south coast that reported to 11 Group Filter Room from the outbreak of war, and even the colour of their plots.

This was the quality of the young women I would have the privilege of working with. Mary Hogg (a niece of Lord Hailsham), Zoe Hicks (offspring of Augustus John), and Pat Robins (daughter of the romance writer Denise Robins) were others who had pioneered the essential work of the Filter Room. All were to become colleagues and good friends. Working underground for long hours of duty in sometimes intense and difficult conditions, complete co-operation and understanding were essential. I was to spend the next eighteen months in their company.

Immediately after checking in at the admin office in the Priory I was taken to join the duty watch in the *Hole,* the underground building where the Operations and Filter Rooms were situated. Initially sited in the ground floor of the Priory, it was soon realised that the special operations block would be a likely enemy target and needed greater protection. After extensive excavations in the grounds to a depth of forty two feet, a bunker was constructed. All these vital operations were moved there in

March 1940. Like other underground facilities, air conditioning and heating were not as advanced as today and conditions could get very uncomfortable – sometimes too hot and, during the times when bad weather meant little air activity, extremely cold. This was the third underground area that I would work in so I knew what I would face.

It was early evening on that first occasion. The table was full of tracks. I could see several squadrons of Bomber Command massing and heading for Germany, interspersed with hostiles, obviously the Luftwaffe's fighters. Our own fighter squadrons were accompanying the bombers to the limit of their range. Patrolling the Channel to the west were Coastal Command aircraft on U-Boat watch. Plotters and Filterers were bent over the table, intent on their work.

The scene was riveting. At last we were fighting back. There was little time to talk, everyone was busy. I stood there absorbing the atmosphere. Despite all the activity on the table and a constant buzz of voices, there was an air of calm concentration. The discipline was impeccable. Every person there seemed to know exactly what they were doing – the Plotters, repeating the information from the Radar stations: 'Fighter 2461 now ten plus aircraft at fifteen. New track showing IFF.'

The Controller from above was calling out as new information appeared: 'Make that new track a fighter, change X raid 286 to hostile.'

From the other side of the balcony I could hear the clearly enunciated voice of the teller, repeating the filtered information to the Group and Sector Operations Rooms, Observer Corps, American war room – to all who need know. 'New track, Roger X-ray, fife niner, two three, fife niner, two three, showing IFF, ten plus at twenty.' No-one ever said five or nine but always fife and niner so these two numbers could not be misunderstood.

During a lull in proceedings, I was taken to meet the duty Controller. Squadron Leader "Rosy" Lee was on duty that night and he was charming. 'Welcome to the Hole,' he said briefly and quickly turned back to look at the table.

Like most of the Controllers, "Rosy" worked pre-war in the stock market. This peacetime work was exactly what was needed for a Controller's task – weighing up information very fast and making a decision, knowing it might be a question of profit or loss – life or death. There had been no time to train people so the RAF made a brilliant decision to recruit from the City of London top bankers, or brokers and jobbers from the Stock Exchange.

At 2000 hours C Watch took over. The changeover took some time, as it was staggered to ensure continuous cover. As I left the bunker at the end of the watch, I realised that I would have to be on top form to work here.

I returned with the others to No. 2 WAAF Officers' Mess, Bentley Manor. It was explained to me that it was a unique place. Because of the security of the work done at Fighter Command Headquarters, those of us on Special Duties were kept apart from the rest of the WAAF officers. There were also eight WRNS officers billeted with us, as they too had top clearance.

Whenever any special women officers visited Fighter Command Headquarters, they would be sent to stay here. On the occasion of a visit by "Bomber" Harris, his personal assistant spent two nights in our Mess. I imagined they thought she might talk in her sleep and let out details of some secret mission.

We left the grounds of Bentley Priory and walked about a quarter of a mile down Stanmore Hill passing the common. The four other Filterers on B Watch were very friendly and said that as it was so late, I was to use the bedroom of someone on leave. They explained that all the rooms in the Mess were currently occupied and another house had been requisitioned a little farther down the hill in Heriots Close. I could go down there the following morning. However, they assured me that most of my time would be spent in the Mess itself.

Although it was very dark when we arrived, I could make out the outlines of a lovely thatched house. We entered through a small garden and went into a large room full of oak beams, with an enormous inglenook fireplace and a roaring log fire. There were well-used armchairs and pictures on the wall. This was our anteroom. It oozed warmth and hospitality. I had a good feeling about this posting.

We joined the other off duty officers for dinner and I was introduced. The PMC (President of the Messing Committee) was Flight Officer Grogono whom I had already met. There were about twenty of us in all at that first meal together. I was told all their names and where they worked. Every one was either Ops or Filter with the exception of the WRNS officers and a Northern Irish Medical Officer. She was the only non-Special Duties officer there but had been seconded to the Mess to keep her eyes open for any signs of stress or sickness amongst us, as every specially trained officer was needed to be available for duty.

I cannot remember much about the meal but I remember what happened afterwards. I was officially inducted into the Mess, standard procedure for all new members. The ceremony entailed me removing my lisle stockings and heavy black shoes, and putting a foot in some blackened ash previously culled from the fireplace and allowed to cool. Then several of my fellow

Filterers turned me upside down and firmly pressed my footprint on the ceiling, joining many others already there. I added my signature. I was now one of them and we would go through a lot of good and bad times together.

It had been a long day. I slept soundly. After breakfast the leader of B Watch, Joan Hargreaves, took me down to my new quarters. It was a modern comfortable house with a couple of bathrooms and several large bedrooms. I found that I would be sharing with two others, Elaine Owrid and Vera Everatt. I had yet to meet them as they were on C Watch. I unpacked and wrote a letter to George giving him my new address.

The few letters I had received from him were arriving in the form of airgraphs. These were introduced because otherwise heavy cargoes of letters would have to be brought back to Britain by sea, from our troops serving overseas, entailing unnecessary risk for the Navy. Consequently all letters were photographed and then airlifted home. Of course this meant a lack of privacy but, as servicemen's letters were always censored, it didn't make much difference and we received them more quickly. Back home the negatives would be printed on special paper and posted to the recipients.

Immediately I received the first airgraph, I realised that George was serving overseas. He could say little about what was happening or where he was, his letters consisted mostly of endearments and telling me he was well and missed me. At least I knew he was still alive.

I had surmised that he was in the Middle East and guessed he was part of the 7th Armoured Division, better known as The Desert Rats. He was serving with the Corps of Military Police. I realised from the news reports he must already have seen several actions in the last few months. I knew that the MPs were in the forefront, directing the mobile units and I hoped he was safe.

B Watch went on duty at midnight. This would be my baptism of fire. I remember it was once more a busy night with a large bombing raid going out to the Ruhr industrial area. We took over as they were due to return. Instead of a large formation, they came back in small groups. This meant there had been a lot of counter action, artillery barrage and German fighter attack. We lost a lot of bombers and crews that first night. I looked at the Plotters.

Despite the problems and the obvious casualties, the girls showed no emotion but just kept on with their task. We knew which squadrons had set out on the mission and many of these young women had connections with several of the bomber crews. I was impressed by their discipline and dedication to the work they knew was vital to ensure the safe return of the stragglers. I understood a lot of tragedy had been and would continue to be enacted in this key room.

By 0200 hours things had started to quieten down and the odd relief was given to both Plotters and Filterers. They went to the canteen nearby for a quick drink and then back to their posts again in under fifteen minutes. By 0500 hours activity on the table started once more. This time it was Coastal Command on their routine patrols and an occasional hostile would appear, perhaps dropping mines in our home waters. This is how it would be – intense activity, a lull, and then back to more activity.

My first watch at Stanmore was over. I had managed to satisfy the eagle eye of Mary Hogg, the Filter Officer on duty. She sat on the balcony and it was her job to pick up errors and delays in keeping tracks up to date or to point out if anyone had missed the appearance of a new track. I had the feeling of being part of a wonderful team.

During the next few days I got to know all the members of No. 2 WAAF Officers' Mess. They were an interesting band of young women from diverse backgrounds. My two bedroom companions at Heriots Close were typical of the mix of people who might never have come together in peacetime. Vera Everatt had come over from the Argentine with her sister Dora; their brother was already serving in the RAF as a pilot. Their father, an agricultural scientist, had been sent there to advise the Argentine Government on suitable crops to be grown in the River Plate delta. His two daughters had lived there from an early age and spoke both English and Spanish fluently.

They wore a flash on their shoulders, BLAV, British Latin American Volunteers. I was amused to learn that although proud of their BLAV flashes, they took them off later after hearing some airmen call out: 'What does that mean? Bloody Lavatories!'

Elaine Owrid was a Scottish lass from Aberdeen whose family had been in the antiques business. She was a great designer and needlewoman and in quiet times in the Filter Room would have the whole watch sewing. They would make blouses out of dusters sewn together or dish cloths out of knitted string and occasionally French knickers out of salvaged parachute silk. After the war, she put her talents to great use and designed ranges of underwear for many famous firms, ending up as a Director with Courtaulds.

Jill Hudson was a well-to-do farmer's daughter from East Anglia, Naomi Westbury a qualified psychiatrist, Joan Hargreaves was from the Home Counties and would meet a Norwegian Pilot, marry him and become Mrs. Ravn, and so it went on – a polyglot collection and I liked and admired them all. We were not short of glamour in the Mess either. Pauline Maguire and June Clapperton, both working in the Ops Room, were C.B. Cochran's Young Ladies and had appeared in many of the Cochran Revues and cabaret at the Trocadero with Jessie Matthews.

Another of the officers working with the Movements Liaison team, Phil Carlebach, was a well-known hockey player and before the war had played many times for England. On hearing that I had played for Southgate County Old Scholars, she immediately arranged for me to have a try-out and before long, I was a member of the Fighter Command team. If it fitted in with off duty times, I would join the team for matches against nearby clubs. It was good to have this exercise after being underground for so many hours.

As the weeks went by I became accustomed to working in the *Hole,* so it was a great surprise to us all to learn that in August 1943 our Filter Room was to be moved above ground into the garden of Hill House, a large mansion that had been taken over by the RAF. Since we were a vital link in the defence of the most heavily bombed area of Britain and a likely target ourselves, we found it hard to understand why this was happening. One end of the Filter Room consisted of a wall of glass upon which all aircraft movements plotted by the Observer Corps were shown. This would have caused enormous injury to personnel if it had shattered. However, we still had to move.

It was only later we found out the reason. Our old premises underground were needed for the high-ranking officers who even then in 1943 were planning the D-Day landings. I guess they were considered more important than us, but even now I cannot understand why the Operations Room was not moved as that could have been duplicated easily if bombed, whereas all our direct lines to Radar stations on the vulnerable south coast would have been destroyed.

There was a slight advantage to us. Hill House was situated midway between our Mess at Bentley Manor and Heriots Close where many of us were billeted so we did not have to walk so far on a cold early morning after a tiring night watch. We did however lose the facilities of the excellent underground canteen in the *Hole* and instead had to walk across a large lawn when we had a break and climb to the third floor of Hill House to the small and ill-equipped canteen there. The choice of refreshment was limited – I can only remember tired Spam sandwiches and the more unusual chopped raw cabbage and Marmite. But at three o'clock in the morning anything was welcome.

Mostly About George

I never thought when I read the airgraph from George, which arrived during the summer of 1943 that it would be the last ever. It had been forwarded to me from 10 Group. Several weeks passed and I heard no more, but I was used to this. I knew that the Military Police moved up with the advancing troops and that the battles in North Africa were now mostly over. The Allies were in control and Hitler defeated. There were rumours of our armies preparing to land in Italy.

I had plenty to do at Stanmore, learning the positions and capabilities of the Radar stations reporting to us and adjusting to the pressures of the amount of air activity. Of course we were not on duty all the time. We worked hard and we played hard. There were parties in our Mess and constant invitations to activities at No. 2 RAF Officers' Mess in another large house about a hundred yards up the hill from us. It was called *The Cedars* and owned by the toothpaste family, the Macleans, but taken over by the Air Force.

All the most senior (and stuffy) officers were housed in No. 1 RAF Officers' Mess in the Priory. No. 2 was full of RAF Filter and Ops Officers.

We were also regular attendees at Lady Reading's Sunday afternoon tea dances at the Grosvenor Hotel if we were off-duty. There we would entertain many of the overseas officers as well as

Army, Navy and RAF personnel, dancing to the music of the famous RAF dance band, *The Squadronaires*. This was Glenn Miller-type music and we would dance Foxtrots, Quicksteps and of course Swing, with the occasional Jitterbugging when any American officers turned up. I was not too good at the latter and Lady Reading showed slight disapproval too. She was a great old lady and would attend almost every Sunday and sit in state surveying the scene.

Central London was so near – just a Tube ride from Stanmore Underground station. The theatres were now open again and we would receive free tickets for shows every week. On several occasions I was able to visit the ballet at Sadler's Wells, and had the opportunity to watch Robert Helpmann, the talented Australian dancer. We were never at a loss for something to do. In fact it was sometimes difficult to find time to sleep.

Although I looked on George as a permanent part of my future life since we had now become unofficially engaged, I had several other men friends and would have meals out or go to the theatre with them. But it was all quite innocent. On the whole we were all pretty naive compared with today's youth. But when Christmas came and I still had no news from George, despite sending regular letters, I began to worry.

One day in early January 1942, I received a letter written in a hand I did not recognise, with a British stamp. The news it contained came as a great shock. It was from George's younger sister, Mary. I thought at first she was writing to say he had been killed, but no – she was breaking the news to me that George had married in Cairo. I was dumbfounded. Why had he not written to me himself?

As part of the 7th Armoured Brigade, he had been in action at El Alamein, where he had been wounded. After a stay in a field hospital he had been sent to Cairo for convalescence. His sister did not say how badly he had been wounded. There he had met an ATS girl working with the Royal Corps of Signals. Her name was Madge.

I knew that during the North Africa campaign, many soldiers were sent back to Cairo for short breaks, and I wondered whether he may have met her previously and they had got together again. Events had moved swiftly. She found herself pregnant and on learning this, George had married her before returning to the Provost Corps. Madge had immediately been dismissed from the Service and returned home to Britain. Mary had taken on the job of looking after her until the birth of the child.

After the initial shock had worn off, I began to understand and perhaps forgive him. As a Territorial aged eighteen, he had been called up a few days before war broke out and was sent with the British Expeditionary Force to France where he endured some heavy fighting. After acting as beachmaster at Dunkirk, he had returned home for a very short time and then had been sent to the Middle East. He had been with the Desert Rats throughout their campaign there, during intense fighting. He had seen considerable losses amongst his fellow soldiers.

Now he was again in the forefront of the battle. And, I thought, she was probably much prettier than me, so I couldn't blame him. After all we had seen little of each other in the last three years. I wrote back to Mary and said I understood and to tell George I wished him luck.

Of course deep down I was very hurt but this sort of break-up was happening all the time. At least I did not have to suffer the heartache of those girls married or engaged to aircrew, girls who daily were getting news that their loved ones were killed in air battles.

My mother was almost more upset than I was. She was very fond of George and already looked on him as a son-in-law. It was not until many years later, when George got in touch with me in 2004, that he told me she had written to him in very angry terms. That evening on the phone he admitted he deserved her rebuke.

It was then I asked him why he had not written to me himself. His answer was brief. 'I was ashamed.' I learned he had been in the Italy landing where he was once more injured and finally had arrived in Berlin where he was part of the occupying force.

I never did ask him whether he was happy. Sadly his wife suffered a very severe stroke and for many years could neither move nor speak. She had to be hoisted from her bed to a chair each day. His only child Jean had never been in good health and had never married. Finally she developed a wasting cancer.

I think he must have been a good man because he told me all those years later that he would never allow his wife to be put in a home. He continued to look after his wife and daughter for several long years. I would never meet him again but having made contact once more, he would telephone me and we would talk about old times. He told me he spent most of his time with ex-service activities and his Masonic friends. He was President of the local Dunkirk Survivors group.

He would tell me of his problems. Perhaps that helped him to cope since he would never discuss them with his male friends. I think he finally was worn down with the caring and the worry. After not hearing from him at Christmas in 2007, I wrote a note early in the New Year hoping all was well. By March I had not received a reply. I decided to phone, something I never normally did. A strange man's voice answered and said: 'This is Mr. Morgan answering for Jean whilst she is in hospital.' Taken aback, I asked if I could speak to George. There was a long pause and the voice said: 'I am sorry to tell you, George died on Hogmanay.' He was a true Scotsman to the end.

Some weeks later I decided to phone Jean as I thought she might be surprised to have come across my letter and wondered who it was from. I explained I was an old friend, I said no more than that. She sounded delighted to hear from me. I continued to speak with her once a month. By then her mother had been put in a home to be cared for but within eighteen months of George dying I learnt both mother and daughter had also died.

Looking back on those wartime events I have no hard feelings. I was not the only one to lose a fiancé. I learnt the lesson that there is not only one partner in the world destined for each of us. I have met several people since with whom I could happily have spent the rest of my life.

Unexpected Events

Life at Fighter Command Headquarters was never dull. There were always new people arriving, VIPs visiting and totally unexpected events occurring.

After the defeat of the Axis troops at the second battle of El Alamein and the later capture of Tobruk, our Middle East forces were ready to attempt a return to Europe from the south. Successful landings were made in Sicily and then at Salerno on the Italian mainland on September 3rd. A few days later Italy capitulated. This was sufficient to give us all a reason to celebrate, prematurely as it turned out. We saw it as the beginning of the end – the end of the war. We drank to the continued success of our invading forces. I could not but wonder if George was with those troops but then put him out of my mind and joined in the celebrations.

Our in-house Medical Officer Doc Moore, I am afraid, drank a little unwisely on this occasion despite being due to go on duty later that evening. Instead of her looking after our medical needs, this time it was our turn. We rang the duty camp ambulance and asked them to come and collect her! We piled her in the back and hoped there were no serious accidents that night! Very soon afterwards, she was posted to a minor Sector station. We never knew whether her over-indulgence was the cause.

There was plenty of work for us on watch. We had moved down to a three-watch basis whilst we were each given a week's leave. So there was less time in between duties to sleep, eat, play or keep our domestic needs under control. At Stanmore, unlike the male officers, we did not have a batman or woman to look after our laundry or polish our buttons. But at least we did not have to clean our rooms.

It was about this time that I caught up with Kenneth Horne once more. He was now the Officer in charge of the Balloon Command unit at Stanmore. He joined us on several occasions when we had a Mess party. By now his wife Jo had left him for a Polish pilot and he was naturally upset. One day he phoned to say he was being posted to Whitehall to join the Equipment section and suggested perhaps if I were in town, we could meet for a drink. A couple of weeks later I arranged to call at his office at Whitehall. I found he was sharing this office with two other officers. On the door were the names Wing Commander Armitage, Wing Commander Horne and Squadron Leader Murdoch. This is where he met Dickie Murdoch for the first time and was the foundation of their future collaboration on the radio comedy programme *Much Binding in the Marsh*, set in a fictitious RAF station. As I joined them that afternoon, they were doing The Times cryptic crossword. It was already obvious that they were a ready-made comedy team. The wisecracks and jokes were continuous between all three of them.

Some time later, Kenneth suggested that I might like to help them with the odd script as I would know better how WAAF behaved and the language they used amongst themselves. I recall sending a couple of suggestions to them, which I believe they may have incorporated in their programmes. By that time I had been posted once more and never was able to meet Kenneth again. But he was a great character and a lovely man.

As officers, we were given a First Class rail warrant when we went on leave for wherever we wanted to go. Having spent most previous leaves at home in London, I decided to apply for a warrant for a place as far away as possible, to see another part of Britain. I asked for a ticket to the Isle of Skye. It was early autumn and I planned to go via Edinburgh and asked my mother to join me there. We spent two nights together in that beautiful city and decided we would like to visit Dunfermline. I remembered the poem of Sir Patrick Spens:

> *"The King sits in Dunfermline toun,*
> *Drinking the blude-red wine,*
> *O whare will I get a skeely skipper.*
> *To sail this new ship of mine?"*

We were told to take the ferry across the River Forth. Making our way down to the port, a policeman seeing my uniform directed us to a small ferry, already almost full of mostly service personnel. Arriving on the far side of the river, we were met by a Military Policeman who surprised me by asking us for our passes. I replied: 'But we're going to Dunfermline.'

He informed us we had taken the wrong ferry. This ferry was taking Service personnel and their families to the Sunday church service at Rosyth Dockyard – a very secret place. Consternation all round, but having checked my details and decided I was not a spy, arrangements were made for us to take another small ferry up the river to the correct quay.

After my mother returned to London, I took a further train to the Kyle of Lochalsh and shared the journey with a Fleet Air Arm pilot going on to Skye. We travelled together on the ferry and landed up in a small hotel at Portree on the island. It was a lovely break and my first introduction to the Scotland that I had heard so much about from George.

Back on duty I discovered that we were making more and more bombing raids on Germany. "Bomber" Harris was increasing missions aimed at tactical targets. By now the United States Air Force was also operating in ever increasing numbers.

When the USAAF pilots first started operations in Europe they were sent on a night exercise called *Operation Bulldog* to evaluate their navigation capabilities. They were sent out over the North Sea. It was a disaster. On their return they lost their way completely. They were spread around the sky trying to find their home bases. It was understandable. The vastness of the United States terrain and the great distances between many of their cities and towns was entirely different from the geography of Britain where one town almost spills on to the next. The decision was made that from then onwards they would operate during the day and the RAF at night. At least then they would see the towns below them!

It was during the winter months that the thatch on the roof of No. 2 WAAF Officers' Mess caught on fire! We always had a roaring log fire in the inglenook fireplace and one afternoon the beam must have become so heated that it caused the thatch to ignite. Two of us climbed on to the roof with fire extinguishers. They were quite difficult to turn on. Mary Hogg eventually got hers started but inadvertently pointed it in my direction and the back of my uniform jacket and skirt were soaked.

There was no time to change so having put out the fire we went straight on duty. About half an hour later, to my astonishment, my skirt disintegrated due to the acid in the extinguisher and it almost dropped off! To preserve my modesty, I was rushed back to the billet to put on a replacement! Fortunately the insurance company paid me for a new uniform.

I was now a firmly established member of No. 2 WAAF Officers' Mess and had been told the secret of Lottie Crump, a newly arrived Section Officer who was attached to B Watch. We told the male officers what a great girl she was – and most attractive. They were all anxious to meet her but they never did. She never seemed to turn up for watch duties, though her footprint appeared on the ceiling of the anteroom, duly signed.

The fact was she never existed. We had invented her, and we kept up the pretence for over two months. We always had excuses for her non-appearance – she would be off on a special course, she was in sick bay, the head admin officer wanted to see her! We even told Pilot Officer Jack Green, a particularly naive *wingless wonder* who was Green by name and *green* by nature, that she could not come on duty one night as we could not get her out of the bathroom where she was enacting an exercise to scuttle the Vichy Fleet. And he believed us! Finally we posted Lottie off to another Filter Room.

All the men who were Filterers were over thirty-five. At that time, no person other than medicos, accountants, padres or scientists were commissioned under that age – unless they were aircrew. We did not have much faith in these men. We thought they were too slow. When we were particularly busy these older male Filterers did not have swift enough reactions in comparison with the WAAF, who were mostly under twenty-two, so the men were taken off the table at busy times, causing immense delight to us all.

Whenever possible we were sent on special visits to bomber stations. The idea was that we could let the crews know how Radar worked to guide them home and emphasise the importance of turning on their IFF booster. I spent three days at RAF Scampton. This was the home of the Dambusters, 617 Squadron. There was a great difference between bomber pilots and the fighter pilots. They were not daredevils since their job needed different skills. The crew worked as a team and their flights were very much longer. They had to face searchlights probing the skies, continuous anti-aircraft activity as well as fighter interceptions.

On another occasion, I was sent to an Air Sea Rescue station to see how our information was used. Fighter Command Filter Room had a close liaison with the Dover station. We always gave first priority to tracks showing the Broad IF Mayday signal and I was anxious to see how they responded. I went out in one of the high speed launches used for picking up the ditched crews. The service was run by the Royal Air Force. The boats were very fast and had a crew of three. They were often escorted by a Lysander aircraft, guiding them to the rescue site but they had no idea of how the location had been calculated by the Filter Room.

Despite long hours on duty, we had a great social life. Often we would go up to London with Zoe Hicks, who had many interesting connections. We would meet her father, Augustus John, at the Cafe Royal where he would be in discussion with other artists and occasionally literary personalities. One special friend of his was Dylan Thomas, though sadly I never met him. I only found out recently that Dylan's wife Caitlin once had been the mistress of Augustus John when he painted her. It would have been interesting to see the two men together.

Recently I had met Sergeant Quentin Baillie, another Scot, this time from Dundee. He was attached to a nearby army ack-ack unit. He was a serious young man a few years older than I was. He loved history and poetry and wanted to travel. We often met in London and would make plans to see the world together at the end of the war. I occasionally took him home when I had a day off and he and my mother became good friends.

When we first met he was in the Royal Army Service Corps. Later he told me he was moving to other duties, which he would never tell me about. Eventually he was posted away and after a while his letters stopped. Once more I went through the agony of wondering if another good friend had been killed. This time I had not taken too seriously our plans for the future. I had learned that this was not wise.

Arriving home unexpectedly for a twenty-four-hour pass, my mother met me with the words: 'Sit down. I have something I have to tell you.' Her face had already warned me that it was not good news. 'I received a letter from Quentin this morning,' she said and handed it to me.

He wrote to say he had been serving with a Special Operations Unit. On one of their forays over to the coast of France he had been seriously wounded – so badly that he would be permanently crippled. He wrote in the letter: 'I would only be a burden to Eileen. I want you to break the news to her. I will never contact her again. This is the best thing. I thank you both for your friendship.'

Once more someone passed out of my life. Since then I have tried every means possible to find out what happened to him, without success. Not being a close relative, I was unable to obtain any military information and I did not know how to contact his family in Scotland. I told myself again: 'No more serious relationships.'

On several occasions Filterer Officers had been sent to Bawdsey Manor to instruct new male Filterers who were now needed for overseas postings. These men were quite a bit older than ourselves and did not always take easily to being taught by a young woman. Late in 1943 I was told I was to be posted there for a month for this purpose. I had a particularly difficult group to teach, including the Managing Director of a well-known clothing company. He had no chance of passing the test and he knew it. He came to me one evening and offered me £50 if I would pass him. I was appalled and explained that passing him would put pilots' lives at risk as well as civilians. He was not at all pleased.

Whilst on that tour of duty, all the women at Bawdsey had to take lessons in shooting. We were now wearing battledress and, with our short hair, we would have been likely targets in the event of an invasion. We were given a Bren gun and taken over to the cliff's edge where we shot out to sea. This practice continued for several days. It was difficult to see how accurate we were. The fishermen were reported to have sent in a complaint as they were being peppered, even though they were considered out of range! All I can remember is that my hip was extremely bruised.

That part of the Suffolk coast was considered a likely spot for enemy landings, especially because of the Radar site there. Later there were reports that burned bodies had been found in the sea, and that the sea had been set on fire. Nothing official has ever been admitted, so it is impossible to know what the truth was.

A new year dawned. 1944 would bring many changes in aerial warfare. There was a constant need to update our fighter and bomber aircraft. New types of Radar instrumentation were being invented. AI (Air Interception), giving fighter aircraft close vision of hostile targets – GCI (Ground Controlled Interception), for inland tracking instead of relying only on Observer Corps observation and sound reports – and new navigational aids such as *Oboe,* used primarily by the Pathfinder Force to locate bombing targets, and *Gee,* giving a fix on target location. The CH Radar stations had been supplemented by Chain Home Low and Extra Low equipment, which increased detection of low flying aircraft. British scientists had been very busy.

All these improvements cost vast sums of money and the government launched a national savings programme called *Wings for Victory*, encouraging the public to buy savings stamps and certificates to provide extra funds.

Fighter Command HQ issued a notice in Daily Routine Orders, asking all watches to organise a public event to advertise the programme. A prize of £200 of savings certificates would be awarded to the watch raising the most savings from the public. B Watch had a meeting and decided to run a garden party in the grounds of Hill House. I was asked to head the campaign.

The grounds around the Filter Room were extensive and offered many opportunities. We formed a committee of two airwomen, one RAF sergeant, another WAAF Officer and myself and we put our heads together to come up with some ideas. We fixed the date for a Saturday afternoon in May and prepared posters telling the public of the event. We emphasised that they could not lose! Whatever they paid for, they would receive the equivalent value in savings stamps and a booklet to complete.

We contacted local shopkeepers and companies in the vicinity and had a great response with offers of many items as prizes for the raffle. We borrowed equipment and tables for an open air tea room. There was a flower bed prepared with a hidden treasure in it where the punters staked their claim. We found a hoop-la and a shove-halfpenny board; there were balloons to let off with children's names on them. We borrowed items from the Scouts and from anyone who had a dart board or skittles.

Yola Kessler, one of the WAAF, who had a tinge of gypsy blood in her veins, offered to tell fortunes. This was to prove one of the most popular attractions of all. There was a lake in the grounds with a small island in the middle. Two WAAF who were keen rowers offered to ferry customers in a small dinghy to Gypsy Yola's tent, erected on the island.

I had noticed a riding school opposite the house, with small ponies as well as larger horses. I decided to call and ask if the proprietor would consider loaning two ponies and perhaps a stable-girl to offer rides for the children. I did not envisage the difference to my life that visit would make.

I knocked tentatively on the door of the house adjoining the Stanmore Riding School. A middle-aged man answered. I guessed he was the owner. He was dressed in breeches and riding boots and had a weathered complexion. 'Can I help you?' he asked. He probably thought I was coming to book a ride. I explained we were trying to raise funds for the Wings for Victory campaign and I wanted his help. He immediately invited me in to discuss the idea and to meet his wife Tommie and her three miniature poodles.

Captain Jimmy Younghusband, known to all as "The Captain", was most enthusiastic. He had served in the Cavalry in

World War One with the Inniskilling Dragoon Guards and promised to do anything he could to help. He offered to provide two quiet children's ponies and also to advertise the event to his clients. Sure enough, on the day the two ponies arrived, Smokey and Bess, together with two seventeen-year-old grooms only too eager to take part.

The day dawned. The weather was kind and the sun shone. We charged an entry fee of one shilling (5p) and most events cost sixpence to enter. That was a lot of money in 1944. But everyone received a savings stamp of equivalent value. The public poured in. Due to wartime restrictions there was not a lot of entertainment available and they were delighted to have somewhere to go on a Saturday. At the end of a busy afternoon, we presented the many raffle prizes provided by local shopkeepers and we thanked the public for their support. It was time to count the takings.

We were amazed. It was considerably more than we had expected. We had raised £556, about 450 people had attended and now they had all started to "Save for Victory". The organising team and the watch were delighted; we had all put so much into the event. We were even more pleased three weeks later when we were told B Watch had raised the most money and had won the £200 saving certificates.

After consultation we decided to donate these to the family of a fighter pilot who had been killed. We made enquiries and contacted the Bluecoat School near Horsham, who had recently awarded a scholarship to a boy and a girl, children of a sergeant fighter pilot who had been shot down during the Blitz. Having found these children, B Watch kept in touch with them until the end of the war, sending them birthday and Christmas gifts. It was a very happy outcome after a lot of effort by the whole of the watch.

The fund-raising event was to have an even greater effect on my own life. A few days after the garden party, I went over to the riding school to meet the owner again. I wanted to thank him for all his help and let him know how well we had done and how much the pony rides had raised. The children loved them and were queuing all afternoon for rides.

I was invited in for a cup of tea and met his son Peter, who was on a 48-hour leave from nearby RAF Northolt where he was currently stationed. Having volunteered for air crew in the very early days of the war, he had failed on his Morse test and was now a non-commissioned officer PTI (Physical Training Instructor). He was also the drummer in the RAF station dance band.

We chatted for a while and he suggested I should book the band for the next dance we would run in the Mess. I told him I would consider it. His father mentioned that there were two large spring ponds in his grounds, which were wonderful for swimming. If any of us from the Mess wanted to use the facility we only had to ask. A week later several of us took up the offer.

It was a warm June day after a tiring night watch and we made our way across the fields near Stanmore Common. We wore our bathing suits under our uniform. We stripped off and dived in. The water was ice cold but so refreshing. Back on dry land we soon fell asleep on the grass. About half an hour later we heard someone say: 'Hello, there. Enjoy your swim?' It was Peter, once more home for a few hours. And that is how it all began.

A Year of Change

During those first five months of 1944, it just seemed to be another year of war with some successes and some setbacks. The war with Japan in the Far East had begun to turn in favour of the Allies but Europe was still occupied. By now we had air superiority in Europe and the German population was facing the heavy bombing casualties that our cities had suffered.

Activity in the Filter Room remained consistent. We were busy both day and night with bombing missions and now there were more and more sorties by Foto Freddies, the name given to the reconnaissance planes based at RAF Benson. The squadron consisted mostly of Mosquitoes with their longer range and extra speed. They had been stripped of their armaments and equipped with the most sophisticated camera equipment. They would fly at over 40,000 feet and at more than 400 mph.

During the early months of 1943 R.V. Jones, a scientist and Deputy Chief Officer of Intelligence throughout the war, had been monitoring messages intercepted and decoded by Bletchley. Initially they were considered to be of no great significance but, on investigation, he realised they were pointing to special test activities at Peenemunde on the Baltic. He believed these were trials of a new type of aerial warfare threatening Britain. Peenemunde was kept under constant photographic surveillance from then on.

On 22nd April 1943 the first photo interpretation of a rocket propelled weapon was observed. On June 23rd 1943 a photographic interpreter, Flight Officer Constance Babington-Smith in the Allied Photographic Intelligence Unit, spotted from photographs taken of the area by the Mosquito Foto Freddies, four little tail-less aeroplanes being launched. On the 12th June, R.V. Jones himself, after a sortie, found the first indication of the threatened vengeance V weapons. This appeared to indicate that the Germans were experimenting with some sort of rocket-launched craft.

On November 13th further photos indicated that launch areas for a flying bomb were being prepared in the Pas de Calais area. This research resulted in preparation for *Operation Crossbow*, which would cover all counter operations against possible launch sites. Lord Haw-Haw had already reported on his nightly broadcasts that Hitler was preparing a secret weapon to annihilate Britain. We were not given full details of these experiments but we were told to look out for any unusual signs of air activity. Thanks to Jones and Babington-Smith, resulting bombing missions to Peenemunde and the Pas de Calais delayed the launch of these new weapons by many months.

It was obvious to us from both RAF and Army manoeuvres in the south of England that something big was brewing. Reports of preparation by the Allies for the invasion of Europe were increasingly heard. The Luftwaffe was sending over their own photo-reconnaissance planes daily, obviously trying to find out where any possible landings might take place.

We had heard from the Radar stations around the Kent and Sussex area that a large amount of camouflaged military equipment was massed in the fields of their coastal hinterland. What few of us knew was that these were all dummies made of cardboard and other materials to mislead the Germans into thinking that the landing would be in the Pas de Calais area. It was the obvious place, with the shortest sea journey across the Channel. We would listen to the news avidly and conversation in the Mess invariably turned to when it would happen. We knew it meant that we would be on high alert.

I had been for several afternoon swims in the Spring Ponds, sometimes with other officers and sometimes alone. I had met

Peter once or twice and we had become quite friendly. I found him amusing and interesting. He was very keen on wildlife and seemed to know a lot about the countryside. His father's fields were on the edge of Stanmore Common, a large area of untouched land.

On this particular sunny afternoon, I was glad to see he too was off duty and about to swim as I wanted to let him know we had decided to book the Northolt station dance band for a party later in the month. It was now June. He was delighted and asked if I would like to meet him that evening for a drink in the Abercorn. This was a pub much frequented by the RAF, half way down Stanmore Hill. It was also the haunt of Bill Hooper, a RAF Flight Lieutenant who was a cartoonist by profession and who was part of the team producing the official RAF magazine called *TM* – short for Training Manual.

This magazine was a light-hearted way to draw attention to aircrew of things they should remember not to do when flying. Bill drew a monthly cartoon featuring Pilot Officer Prune who never did anything right. The Abercorn pub walls were adorned with Bill's original drawings. I particularly remember one cartoon featuring P.O. Prune in his aircraft underwater, with fish peering into the cockpit and the plane festooned in seaweed. The caption underneath read: 'The day when P.O. Prune failed to pull out of his dive in time.' Prune became a famous RAF institution.

Having agreed to go for a drink, I told Peter I would have to be there early in the evening and would only stay for half an hour as I needed a couple of hours sleep before I went on duty at midnight. That evening I found Peter an entertaining companion, a great raconteur and very attractive. About six inches taller than me, he had slightly wavy brown hair and blue eyes and was obviously quite athletic.

He told me he had volunteered for air crew in the early days of the war, as he had been brought up with the de Havilland boys, sons of the founder of the well-known aircraft company. When

170

they were growing up, Peter's father let them have free rides on his ponies and in return Peter would go to Hendon with them and fly in various aircraft there.

When he was training for air crew he managed to pass all the exams with one exception – learning the Morse code. In those early days there were so many volunteers for flying duties that failure in any one area meant you were not accepted. He told me he was very disappointed as he had always wanted to be a pilot, having once met the famous Amy Johnson who was learning to ride, as this was to make her hands more responsive when flying.

Instead he was posted to RAF Cosford to train as a Physical Training Instructor and then posted to RAF Northolt. Since the PTI department also covered troop entertainment, his pre-war hobby as a drummer in a semi-pro dance orchestra led him to join the Northolt station dance band. During that short time with him that evening, I learnt a lot more about him and I realised I was becoming rather interested in this young man.

On the stroke of midnight B Watch reported for night duty. As we took over from the outgoing watch, we had no idea how important our work would be that night. The handover was always very swift as no time could be lost. We had immediately to assess the information on the table and take over the duties of collating, recalculating positions and identifying the aircraft tracks. We had to assimilate the current state of operations instantly. The majority of the personnel working that night in the Filter Room were young women – the Filter Officer, Plotters, Tellers, Raid Orderly, Movements Control team as well the Filterers. This was a woman's war.

That night it was obvious that something unusual was happening. The overhead balcony where the Controller sat was unusually full – swamped with gold braid. Army Generals, Naval Commanders and high-ranking Air Force Officers were staring intently at the table below. As we looked at the table, we could see it was not only full of aircraft tracks, but the English Channel was also full of naval craft. As Section Officer Doreen Seligman handed over to me, she whispered: 'It's started.' Operation Overlord had begun. The date was June 6th 1944.

Threats and Promises

It was the most anxious yet exhilarating eight hours of my life as we worked that night when the Allied Forces returned to the mainland of Europe. Radar tracked the Navy carrying the troops to the beaches of Normandy. As the hours went by we plotted the RAF fighters in action over the north French coast, followed by a slower force towing gliders full of paratroops. We could only imagine what was happening in France. We were astonished that there were not more signs of hostile aircraft. Had the decoy strategy worked? Certainly there was more enemy activity in the Pas de Calais area.

By dawn we received news that despite heavy gunfire several of the landing areas were being secured. There were however reports of heavy opposition at Omaha beach where the American troops were landing. This beach was covered in anti-tank and anti-landing craft obstacles. One of the only remaining first class front line infantry divisions available to the Germans was also guarding the beach, purely by coincidence. This made the assault the most difficult of all the beaches on D-Day, earning the nickname "Bloody Omaha". By now, the Stukas were bombing the troops landing.

The other landings had been more successful. We were getting reports through the night that the Allies had gained a foothold once more on the Continent. As we went off-duty at 0800 hours, we felt we had played a small part in one of the

173

greatest military operations of all time. It was still far too early to be sure how successful Operation Overlord would be. Several days would pass before the nation could be sure that the German forces were in retreat.

After breakfast that morning we were too excited to sleep. Many of us had a husband, a fiancé, a brother or cousin who we guessed would be amongst the forces either already landed in France or following soon after, so it was joy mixed with apprehension. Despite what had happened, I couldn't help wondering whether George was in the initial landings.

Needless to say everyone in the Mess kept close to the radio for the latest bulletin. Despite the initial setback on Omaha, within a few days the entire beach had been transformed into an artificial harbour, code-named Mulberry. As the days passed in that first week, we would ask the watch coming off duty how things had gone. We felt part of Overlord. We were optimistic about the outcome.

Those June days were fine and warm, and Peter and I would meet for a swim if our time off coincided. We were becoming more than friends. Sometimes I would go back to his house and have a cup of tea with his parents. They were most welcoming but very different from anyone else I had ever met.

The vocabulary of the horsey world was strange to me and the house was constantly invaded by the clients, who ranged from City businessmen to hearty booted county ladies and the occasional film star. "The Captain" had close ties with Denham, Pinewood, and Elstree studios and often provided horses and riders for films. He had been doing this for many years and was known throughout the industry. On occasions he would double for stars unable to ride; for example in *The House of Rothschild* he stood in for George Arliss in one scene.

Peter's mother, known as Tommie to all, came from the Newman family with supposedly distant connections to Cardinal Newman. Her father had served in the Consular Service in places including Puerto Rico and Thailand, then known as Siam. She was definitely *County*. Peter and his brother Derek had been brought up as Catholics and educated at Catholic public schools, The Oratory and Ampleforth, despite their father being the son of a Church of England cleric. Both sides of the family hailed from the Sussex area.

Amazingly, the riding school business was managing to survive despite difficulty in finding feed for the horses. Fortunately the Ovaltine factory in Kings Langley had come to the rescue. Sir Harry Hague, the inventor of this popular drink and proprietor of the company, was a regular member of the Sunday morning ride. To ensure the horses were fed, he offered the spent grains, the residue left from the cereal after the extraction of what was used to make Ovaltine. Twice a week the head stable girl would take the old open Ford and a trailer to the factory and bring back the wet residue. I was learning a lot about horses and their maintenance.

On June 13th, a week and a day after the D-Day landings, once more B Watch was on night duty. It seemed to follow the usual pattern, bomber missions over Germany, constant activity over northern France where the Allies were slowly advancing, missions by Foto Freddies and an occasional calibration exercise.

Shortly before dawn several low flying hostiles were picked up in the Pas de Calais area, approaching at high speed. As one crossed our south coast, the Observer Corps reported there was a flame coming from the rear of the plane. It was assumed it had been hit by the coastal artillery, but it continued flying. They also reported that the sound of the engine was different, a staccato throbbing. As one of these hostiles approached London, suddenly the sound stopped. There was complete silence, followed a few seconds later by a violent explosion. At first it was thought that an ack-ack battery had brought it down. Several of the other tracks disappeared over the Channel and two more came down over open land in Kent.

Very soon it was obvious that these were not ordinary aircraft but Hitler's much vaunted secret weapon, an unmanned flying bomb. Londoners had been free of attack since the end of the winter of 1943/44. Now they would be the target of the V1, an indiscriminate weapon that would detonate wherever it ran out of fuel.

Londoners during the next few months would learn that whilst they could hear the sound of the throbbing engine they were safe; when the sound ceased it was too late to take cover. The explosion would take place in seconds. Designed to terrorise, this new form of attack would cause more deaths and equal destruction to the Blitz at no cost to Germany of valuable aircrew. Despite its horror the Cockneys called it a *Doodlebug* or a *buzz bomb*, a more friendly term belying its devastating effect. The RAF code name was *Diver*. To the Germans, it was V1 – V for *Vergeltungswaffen* – meaning Vengeance weapon.

Anti-aircraft guns were able to shoot them down fairly successfully but it was soon realised that to target them over London would be both pointless and perilous, as they would still explode where they fell. So a new strategy was put in place. The guns were moved down to the coast to shoot the V1s as they approached over the sea. Filter Room advance warning was vital for immediate and accurate gun-laying to be carried out.

Fighter squadrons were also brought into action and the pilots soon mastered the technique of flipping the wings, causing the flying bomb to go off course and explode harmlessly over the sea. Hundreds were downed off the coast of Kent, but supplies of this weapon were so enormous that despite large numbers exploding soon after launch or being shot down, thousands more reached the London area.

It would not be until Allied troops had overrun the area around the Seine estuary and the Pas de Calais by September that the attacks would temporarily stop whilst the launch sites were moved. When they resumed, greater distance meant increasing inaccuracy.

We plotted thousands of V1 attacks by day and night. Many of us had difficulty in sleeping after a particularly busy watch. It was impossible not to think of the suffering they caused. In total it is said that more than 10,000 were launched against Britain. Of these 7,488 reached our coast. 3,957 were destroyed en route and only 3,531 reached London. These still resulted in the deaths of more than 6,000 civilians, with 18,000 wounded.

If R.V. Jones had not investigated those unusual Bletchley Park Enigma intercepts and realised that they related to the testing ground at Peenemunde, the result might have been very different. His foresight ensured heavy bombing attacks on the site during 1943, destroying many of these weapons and delaying their use. Without his brilliance, there would have been disruption of the plans for D-Day and possibly considerably greater military losses.

Stanmore experienced an occasional V1 explosion nearby without too much damage. In the Filter Room, now above ground, we were often anxious when we could see from the glass screen displaying the Royal Observer Corps tracks, a V1 heading our way. This screen covered the whole of one wall and was the height of two storeys of the building. If it had shattered many of the personnel would have been seriously injured, if not killed. Fortunately it survived and so did we.

Meanwhile I spent any spare time I could with Peter. He could get home frequently on his motor bike from Northolt, even if it was only for a few hours. I had taken him over to meet my parents. I wondered how he would react to our humble semi-detached home in a north London suburb but he got on famously with both my mother and father. On one occasion he took my grandfather Tom Smith, a delightful genuine Cockney, to the local pub for a beer. Peter liked his beer and so did my grandfather. My mother seemed pleased that I now had a boy friend less likely to be sent into a fighting zone.

For my birthday, July 4th, Peter asked me to make sure I was off-duty that evening as he had booked for us to go out to dinner at the famous Criterion Restaurant in the West End.

The day arrived. I wore my uniform as we were not allowed to change out of it except when on leave. As we sat down Peter ordered an expensive bottle of red wine. I wondered how he could manage this on a Corporal's pay but I guessed his mother had helped. She idolised her two boys.

As we took our first sip Peter said: 'There is something I want to ask you. Would you marry me?'

Just like that – I certainly had not expected it. Yet it seemed right. Hardly hesitating a moment, I looked at him and said: 'Yes.'

We had met for the first time only seven weeks before. We really knew very little about each other. We had exchanged some ideas, talked a little about our hopes for the future, but we had very few things in common at that time. That is how it was in wartime. So many of my fellow officers have told me that they too rushed into engagements and marriage without knowing much about each other. Sometimes it worked, sometimes it didn't. But when you did not know what the next day would bring, it didn't seem to matter. Here and now was what was important.

A week earlier the subject of precious stones had cropped up in conversation and I had mentioned I was not a great jewellery person but I did love opals with their changing colours. That evening, Peter gave me my engagement ring – a beautiful opal set in platinum in a gold circle. He had talked to Gus Neal, a director of Bravington's, the well-known jewellers, who had produced this one from his coffers. I was delighted. I did not know then that opals brought tears.

The restaurant must have been told of the possibility of me accepting Peter's proposal since they produced a bottle of precious champagne to celebrate. And that was it, a taxi back home and on duty again at midnight, together with my new ring. Everyone noticed it and my special friend, Kay Tanner, in charge of the watch we were relieving, said: 'I didn't think it would be long. You've been spending so much time at the Spring Ponds; I couldn't imagine you went there only for the swimming!'

179

Peter had spoken to my parents on the phone earlier that day and told them he was going to ask me to marry him. He said they seemed very pleased. I guessed they would be, after the other near misses! During the next couple of weeks we decided on September 30th as the wedding day. I agreed to marry in the Catholic Church in Edgware, provided we were able to get a dispensation in time.

If a Catholic wanted to marry a Protestant (or heretic as they were sometimes called!), a dispensation had to be obtained. I went to meet the Priest in Charge, Canon Goggin. He asked me my name and I replied 'Eileen Le Croissette.'

'Ah,' he said smiling, 'One of us!' I had to disillusion him.

'My forefathers were Huguenots from Picardie and were persecuted by the Catholics after the Revocation of the Edict of Nantes in 1698!' I was well genned up on the history of the family. He did not try to convert me and we received the dispensation a week later.

Whenever Peter and I could meet in the next few weeks, we used the time to plan the event. He would wear uniform and I would try and get hold of a wedding dress – how, I had no idea. But Elaine Owrid, my fellow housemate and an amateur seamstress, said she would make it for me if we could scrounge some clothing coupons for the material. Between the two families, we raised enough to buy the necessary yardage. I left it to Elaine to buy and design it, not being very fashion conscious at the time.

Dora Everatt had brought a beautiful lace mantilla from the Argentine that her sister Vera had worn for her wedding. The two girls suggested I too should wear it. I had a pair of black court shoes from my pre-war days, barely used, and was offered the loan of a precious pair of nylons from one of the B Watch airwomen, a present from her American GI boyfriend.

One of the riding school clients owned a hotel in Edgware. The free use of the hall for the reception was their wedding present to us. My mother suggested she and a few of her friends would do their best to provide a buffet for the guests. The guest list was becoming far longer than I had expected. I had several relatives to invite – my parents and my brother, aunts and uncles and especially my aunt from Bath and her family. Of course my friends from the Mess were included, and a couple of old school friends.

The Younghusband family was not large. Peter's parents and his brother Derek, an aunt and an uncle, but there were no cousins living in Britain. However, Peter's parents wanted to invite several of their influential clients. It was going to be quite a mixed gathering. Sir Harry Hague and Sir Frederick Handley Page, plus their wives and family, were invited with about twenty more of the regular Sunday ride clients and of course the staff of the riding school.

The numbers were mounting. I wondered where the rations would come from to feed them all. Peter had already asked Bill Hooper, the RAF cartoonist, to be his best man and my brother and two school friends were delegated as ushers. The invitations were sent out. Peter's mother had managed to find some elegant embossed ones from old stock in a local stationery shop. Everybody seemed free on that date and anxious to come. We received sixty-five acceptances.

That was a lot to cater for on wartime rations. But I had forgotten the Younghusbands had a cow called Blossom that provided plenty of milk and cream. They also had chickens, so there were eggs. Then an offer came from the Head RAF Chef at No.2 Officers' Mess to make the wedding cake. He promised three tiers and a special decoration on the top, but we had to find the eggs, sugar and dried fruit. Things were looking brighter.

Peter's mother notified the Tatler of the wedding and the venue. When they saw that her son was not a commissioned officer – even though I was – they decided they were not interested. Such was the snobbery of the day in some quarters.

Just after the beginning of the war I had a strange encounter. Whilst I was walking down the main road in Winchmore Hill, about to go into one of the shops, a very large, obviously foreign, gentleman with a flowing black moustache stopped me with the words: *'Parlez-vous francais?'*

'Oui,' I replied.

He had with him his petite wife and three children; two teenage daughters and a son slightly older. He explained that he and his family had managed to get on the last boat to leave Ostend as the Germans were marching through Belgium. They were living with other refugees in a house nearby. He had been told to report to the police station but he was finding it difficult as he could not speak English. I offered to help and together we went to the nearby station, where George's father had once been the Inspector. I managed to act as translator for the family and they were overjoyed.

I promised to keep in touch and gave them my home address and phone number. I had seen them several times since then and we had become firm friends. The two girls were now seventeen and eighteen. I thought how nice it would be if they could be my bridesmaids. When I mentioned this to them they were thrilled. Their mother was a keen needlewoman and by devious means managed to acquire enough material to make two charming dresses for the girls ready for the great day.

It was now the end of August. Allied troops were forcing their way through France. Paris was liberated on the 25th. By September 3rd, Brussels too was free. Things were moving fast.

An Eventful Month

I seemed destined to be on duty at times of special significance. In August we had been warned that Germany had been preparing a second secret weapon but we were given no details, except that we might receive a warning message from one of 11 Group Radar stations. *Big Ben* was the code word. On the night of 11th/12th September, B Watch reported for duty. There was little activity on the table. Section Officer Kay Tanner – "Willi" to us all – said as she handed over: 'Not much doing so far, thank goodness. I needed a break!' She was the officer I admired most and recently we had become very friendly. We had both enrolled in a correspondence course, she for journalism and I for poetry.

I took up my place at the table and filtered a few Coastal Command patrols and a fighter exercise off Tangmere. I managed to take a short break at 0430 hours. It was still fairly quiet. At 0745 hours the plotter connected to Swingate jumped up out of her seat, obviously excited: 'Ma'am, my operator has just said "Big Ben" to me three times!'

I realised its importance and that it was up to me to give the signal. I jumped up on a chair and shouted: 'Big Ben, Big Ben, Big Ben!' The effect was instantaneous. The Controller pressed a warning bell, notifying all who were on his list that we had received this signal. The balcony sprang to life, people leaning over to watch the table below, phones ringing. I had no idea at the time that I had announced the first V2 rocket to be launched against London.

After going off watch that morning we did not feel much like sleeping. We were too surprised and upset at the turn of events and we sat discussing what it would mean until almost lunchtime. We realised that despite the successes of the Allies in pushing the Wehrmacht back, Hitler was not giving up easily.

Five missiles had been launched that morning from La Coupole, in the Pas de Calais area still occupied by the German forces. Two had crashed at take-off, two landed on London and one on Paris. This was the beginning of another period of terror for those living in the south-east of England. The first V2 landed at Chiswick, killing three people and causing many injuries. Reports came back that some people had seen what they thought was a rocket and had heard something like a double thunder crack and the sound of a heavy body rushing through the air. No official announcement was made to the public and we of course were sworn to secrecy.

This was the beginning. It would not be until November 10th that members of Parliament were officially told and the public notified that Hitler had launched a second secret weapon. This was forced on the Government since, on the previous day, German propaganda announced that the V2 supersonic rocket had been used successfully against Britain. Since the Allied forces were pushing the Wehrmacht back through the Low Countries, some good news for the German nation was essential to restore morale.

Unknown to us, photo reconnaissance of Peenemunde as early as May 1942 had provided some clues to this weapon. Later a V2 had also gone off course during the testing period and landed in Sweden. Our agents there had managed to secure it and get it back to Britain. A second one misfired in Poland and this too was secreted back for examination. Our scientists went on to develop a method whereby certain Chain Home long-range Radars could detect the initial launch.

Five of the stations in our area had been equipped with the special device called *Oswald* that could pick up this signal. However, the V2 flew at 3,300 m.p.h. at an altitude of up to 50 miles, and took only three minutes to reach its target. A survivor reported that a second after the sound was heard, they would detonate. Despite being aimed at the centre of London, the rockets were very inaccurate. And there was another problem – because artillery shells fired from the French coast gave a similar signal to a V2 launch it was impossible to separate the signals.

The Government was in a dilemma. With no way of identifying where the rockets would hit, it was decided that no public warning would be given.

Originally a plan was devised by General Sir Frederick Pile, Commander-in-Chief of the Ack-Ack Command to provide a constant barrage over the Thames estuary, designed to shoot down the V1s. A barrage of artillery from London's ack-ack units might shoot down some of the missiles – but since they would explode on impact, that was self-defeating. The anti-aircraft guns were subsequently moved to the coast where it was hoped they would then be able to shoot some down over the sea.

Later his plan for *Engagement of Long Range Rockets with AA Gunfire* (gunfire into a radar-predicted airspace to intercept the V-2 rocket) was ready on March 21st, 1945 but the plan was not used due to the danger of shells falling on Greater London.

Unlike the V1, which was launched from a camouflaged ski ramp, which could be easily targeted and bombed, the V2s were fired from mobile launchers that would move out into the countryside, into the woods, to the coast or to city car parks, launch the missile and then move on. During the period when they were operating from France, attempts were made to bomb the launch vehicles. These were unsuccessful, though pilot Raymond Baxter recalled one pilot in his Spitfire squadron shooting at a rocket that had just been fired.

After that initial *Big Ben* warning, reports of launches were diverted to a special unit dispersed from Headquarters and situated on Stanmore Common. Two senior WAAF Officers, Flight Officer Zoe Hicks and my friend Grog were moved there to calculate the launch positions. Neither was particularly good at geometry and the counterattacks were not very successful, so after a couple of weeks they were moved back to the Filter Room.

It was only in recent years when I was again in contact with Grog that she told me what they had been doing, since once more they had been sworn to secrecy. However, countermeasures were being planned and our troops were by now gradually moving into the Low Countries.

As the days passed, more and more of these terrifying missiles both V1 and V2, fell indiscriminately upon London and in Kent. The civilian population were becoming increasingly worried: These weapons were so different from the bombing of the Blitz when people could see and hear the aircraft and recognise that our fighters were up there retaliating. Now there seemed no means of stopping the destruction and the deaths.

At the end of September, V weapon attacks temporarily ceased, as Allied troops had overrun the launch areas in France.

Once the equipment was moved north of Rotterdam the attacks were resumed but frequently failed to reach their target, often landing in East Anglia. It was then that Antwerp became a second target. It was the first large port liberated where the Allies could land troops and supplies. This Belgian city would be the target for over 300 more V2s than London and in a shorter time frame.

Meanwhile my wedding date on September 30th was rapidly approaching. I was told I would be allowed four days leave, but I would have to work the 1600 hours to midnight watch on September 29th, so not much time for beauty sleep! The wedding dress was finished, a last minute booking made for a honeymoon hotel at Rottingdean on the Sussex coast, and a hair appointment for first thing on the morning of the wedding. The service was at 1500 hours, or as the invitation said, 3 p.m. It looked as though everything was under control. Several times I wondered whether I was doing the right thing. I had seen very little of Peter in the last few weeks.

Presents were already arriving at Peter's home, North Lodge, a large family house adjoining the main stable yard. Nothing would be opened before the day. More were arriving at my own home, together with telegrams of good wishes from friends and relations living too far away to attend and from friends in the Forces overseas. It was a hectic few days for the two families.

My evening shift on the 29th was extremely busy. A thousand bomber raid headed for the heartland of Germany with an escort of fighters to the limits of their fuel. As usual, not all our bomber crews returned to base. Once more, we were left to wonder whether they had landed in Germany and been taken prisoner or if the aircraft had crashed in flames. I slept fitfully that night.

I was up in time for a quick breakfast and my hair appointment. Elaine Owrid, efficient as always, was on hand as I dressed in the beautiful gown she had made of figured satin. It fitted perfectly. No wonder she made her name after the war in the fashion industry. Dora stood by with her white lace mantilla. But first I had lunch. It was a lunch I remember, not for its gastronomic elegance, more for its ordinariness! It consisted of brown stew, cabbage and boiled potatoes followed by prunes and custard. Needless to say, I did not eat very much. I hoped the post-wedding buffet would offer something more appetising.

My two Belgian bridesmaids arrived, looking very pretty in matching dresses, with my parents and Dennis. Everyone looked very smart; my father had hired a tail suit for the occasion. Dennis and his fellow ushers were in their best suits. Flight Lieutenant Bill Hooper, the best man, arrived in uniform. The two girls and I left in one wedding car, followed by the family in the second. Time of launch around 1445 hours. A lot of the WAAF officers had gone on in advance in RAF transport.

It was a beautiful late autumn day, the leaves beginning to change colour. My dress was simple but elegant, with just a suspicion of a train. My bouquet of white carnations and chrysanthemums with masses of trailing maidenhair fern gave off a heavy perfume. The hairdresser had done her best with my Service trim and the beautiful white Spanish lace mantilla, fixed firmly to my hair, trailed almost to the floor. I felt ready to face the public.

We arrived promptly on time at the Edgware Church of St. John. My father took my arm as we waited in the porch for the music to begin. As the organist started to play the *Wedding March* we made our way down the aisle. Peter turned and smiled.

I cannot remember much from then on – a sea of faces, Peter in his best uniform and Canon Goggin in his elaborate robes. Since I was not a Catholic the service was mercifully quite brief. I think there was a small choir and the assembled congregation sang vigorously. We exchanged vows but I did not promise to obey. Then it was over except for the civil part of the service. As it was not an Anglican church, the official Registrar had to attend. In a small back room we went through the legal formalities of becoming man and wife. We returned to the church and together walked back up the aisle.

As we stood outside for photographs, there was no confetti and not even any rice – that was needed for food. A few more photos in the grounds of the church and then our car took us a short distance to the hotel owned by the Garrett family. I had no idea what the hall would look like as there had been no time to visit, so I was amazed and delighted to see how everyone had made a great effort to make it quite beautiful.

There were flowers from local gardens and a long buffet table, white clothed and full of an amazing selection of dishes. These were all contributions from friends and family members despite the limits of rationing. The crowning glory was the wedding cake, a wonderful three-tier production topped with a small vase and a white rose. The RAF chef had excelled himself. There was beer and white wine for the guests and plenty of soft drinks, and someone had even produced enough bottles of champagne for the toast. My father gave a short but touching speech, followed by Peter. His also was short but as usual humorous, and finally Bill Hooper thanked the bridesmaids and told them how lovely they looked. I never knew whether their English was good enough to understand.

AN EVENTFUL MONTH

At 1830 hours we left to spend our first night together in a London hotel. The following morning, we took the train for Brighton and a taxi to the Old Close Hotel at Rottingdean. Those three days passed in a flash. We found time to visit Brighton; we walked around Rottingdean, learning about Rudyard Kipling and his life there. We talked, we made love, me for the first time. I don't know about Peter, I never asked him. And then it was over. Both back to Stanmore – no time to open our presents. Peter picked up his motorbike and returned to RAF Northolt, and I went to Heriots Close and changed back into my uniform ready to go on duty at midnight for yet another busy watch.

It would be three days before we met again for a few hours to open our presents, which were waiting for us on the dining table of North Lodge. It was amazing how generous people had been despite shortages and rationing. Many had used their precious coupons for a gift. Sir Frederick Handley Page had exchanged his for two beautiful woollen blankets that I use to this day. Another guest gave us an antique silver coffee pot from the family treasures. There was a china tea set and a dinner service, both Royal Worcester but in white as no coloured china was being made. We were overcome with the kindness of our friends.

We had planned to convert the bothy over the main stable block into a small flat for our use on our days off. Peter had been working on it in his spare time, but I had never seen it. Now I was to be shown it. Up the steep stairs we climbed, past the tack room, to an area above the horse boxes. I opened the door.

My new husband had done a wonderful job. In the tiny kitchen was a table top. Peter lifted it up and there was the bath. The rest of the flat consisted of a small sitting room and two bedrooms. So far there was not much furniture but Peter's father

191

owned two adjoining cottages to accommodate his resident pupils and somehow he had found enough surplus furniture to provide a bed, table and two chairs. Peter had constructed a chest for clothes by nailing together three ammunition boxes. It was a start.

This would be our home for the next two and a half years, but for now we could only use it on the odd occasion when our days off coincided. We moved our wedding presents into the flat, gave it a name for the postal service – *The Studio*. Then we shut the door, kissed goodbye and both went back on duty.

Second Tactical Air Force

The month of September had seen a temporary pause in the V1 and the V2 offensive as the supply bases and underground launching ramps in France were overrun by Allied troops. As the German Army retreated, the V1 and V2 units were hastily relocated in Holland, north of Rotterdam.

On September 2nd Brussels was liberated, followed two days later by Antwerp. This was a major victory since this large port would provide entry for all the necessary supplies and additional troops as the Allies pushed forward into Germany.

However, our forward troops failed to seal off the peninsula, thereby allowing 80,000 German soldiers of the 15th Army to escape and continue the fight. This failure delayed the arrival of any Allied supply ships until November 29th. Our troops had to clear South Beveland and Walcheren before the port could be used. It then took the Royal Navy a further two weeks to remove the mines left by the retreating Wehrmacht.

Unlike the ports of Brest and Cherbourg, destroyed by the retreating German Army, Antwerp had been left surprisingly intact. Realising the vital importance of the port to the Allies, Hitler now ordered all V weapons to target only London and Antwerp and cease all action against French targets. The Belgian port would receive several hundred more V2s than London over a shorter period. The first landed on October 13th causing several deaths and considerable damage.

11 Group Filter Room was crucial in *Operation Crossbow*, the name given to V weapon counter-operations, since all reports from the Radar stations fitted with the special Oswald device were received there. Once Antwerp became the major target, Eisenhower, now in charge of Supreme Headquarters Allied Expeditionary Force, SHAEF, demanded control of the missile warning sources and ordered that all countermeasures were now to be installed on the Continent.

The total force of mobile Radar units – MRUs – together with flash-spotting equipment was sent over to Belgium and on November 19th, 105 Mobile Advance Reporting Unit – MARU – was formed. Then came the surprise. Soon after this date, eight Filterer Officers from 11 Group were ordered to report to the Wing Commander's office. I was to be one of them. We were told we were being sent overseas on a special mission. We had been chosen as we were the most mathematically capable. Although married women were not normally sent overseas I was told I had to go. I could not refuse.

We would have a short training for our new duties and would leave for Belgium early in December, less than two weeks away. We would join 33 Wing of 2nd Tactical Air Force – 2nd TAF – but we would still be reporting back to 11 Group Filter Room. Eight WAAF sergeants together with the Scientific Observer, Flight Officer Ann Richmond, would accompany us. We had already worked with Ann, who was a tall, rather quiet Oxford graduate in her late twenties. The other Filterers included Doreen Seligman, a close friend of Mary Hogg, and Peggy Jones, who was a Canadian volunteer and someone I got on well with.

It was a couple of days before I told Peter I was being posted overseas. I did not want to break the news over the phone. Since returning from our honeymoon we had met only five times. On two occasions we were able to spend the night together in *The Studio*. I knew he would be shocked.

'Why you?' he demanded. I could only say that they needed people who were good at geometry. 'What do you need that for?'

I couldn't tell him but I was able to say: 'I will be going to Belgium. I don't know for how long.' He was desperately upset and could not understand why I would not tell him what I was going to do. I had forgotten in the few weeks I had known him to tell him that I had signed the Official Secrets Act. But even if I had been free to explain, it was impossible as I had no idea myself.

The next two weeks were spent learning how to use a slide rule to extrapolate the trajectory of the V2 flight to find the launch position. We were to be part of a team based at Malines (or Mechelen, as it is called in Flemish), about 12 kilometers from Antwerp. Our job was to use readings from the mobile Radar units of part of the V2 launch curve, combine it with the position where the missile landed and by extrapolation we could then calculate the launch vehicle's position – no computers – just a slide rule and pencil and paper and the knowledge of elementary geometry. We had six minutes in which to do this.

The V2s were placed on a trailer and driven to a secluded site, perhaps in a forest, on the coast, anywhere where they could not be observed. They were then fuelled and winched into launch position. It was estimated it took approximately twenty minutes after launch to dismantle the winching mechanism and load the fuel containers, before moving off and returning to their supply base.

Our calculations, coupled with sound recordings from army survey units, would be passed on to Intelligence. Patrolling Mosquito bombers armed with a torpedo type bomb would then be directed to destroy the launch vehicles. This was a new way of curtailing V2 raids. Since it was almost impossible to stop them once launched, it was hoped this new strategy would destroy the launcher vehicles and gradually eliminate further attacks.

Barely six weeks after our wedding day I kissed Peter goodbye. I was able to give him the address of 33 Wing HQ at Koningin Astridlaan, Malines, but no telephone number. He was very emotional. Perhaps I am made differently. I realised I had been asked to do something which might contribute in a small way to help shorten the war and, if I am honest, I was looking forward to this adventure.

Ironically the transport took us to Peter's base, RAF Northolt, where the aircraft was waiting. Together with the eight WAAF sergeants and several Army Officers, we climbed into a Dakota. It was no luxury aircraft, just a typical troop carrier with seats along each side of the cabin. Our luggage was loaded in the space between our feet. We carried the minimum with us, just personal effects, no civilian clothes and little else. The aircraft was already half full with other RAF personnel and a couple of civilians. We took off into a misty November sky, heading for the Channel.

Less than an hour later we landed at Ghent where we were transferred to waiting RAF vehicles. The officers had the luxury of travelling by jeep; the airwomen went in the usual truck. We set off through the open Belgian countryside past small villages to Malines. It was getting dark as we arrived. We were taken to HQ, which also housed the Officers' Mess. It was an old building in the centre of the town. I noticed a sign above the main door. It said *Soldatenheim* – obviously a place only recently vacated by the occupying German troops

We were welcomed by our new Commanding Officer, Wing Commander Fry. As a Squadron Leader he had been one of the most experienced Filter Room Controllers and most of us had worked with him at one or other of the Group Headquarters. He too was drawn from the Stock Exchange and had been involved in the setting up of 33 Wing from the outset.

After a reviving cup of tea we were given an outline of the set-up. There was no sleeping accommodation in the building so we would all be billeted in private houses. As we were dropped off around the centre of town it seemed mostly to consist of old buildings and had suffered little damage. In 1939 the Wehrmacht had swept through neutral Belgium within hours.

The house destined to be my lodging was owned by Ignace Kennis, who I later found out was a well-known Belgian artist. He and his wife lived in a large terraced house built in the late 1800s. As I was introduced to them, I said: '*Bonjour, enchantée de faire votre connaissance.*' They looked relieved to find I could speak some French as neither spoke English. I would find that normally they spoke Flemish to each other, as did most of the townspeople. We were in Flanders.

On first appearances it did not seem a very welcoming house – large rooms with high ceilings and very cold. All the walls were covered with religious symbols, metal crosses, texts and paintings. The curtains were made of a dark velvet fabric and looked as if they had never been taken down or cleaned.

I was shown my bedroom. The double bed was very old with a huge, ornately carved bed head and covered in a well-worn brown bedspread. I unpacked my case and stored my things away in a vast chest of drawers. This would be the only room I was allowed to use. My hosts told me that as there was a great shortage of food, they would not be able to offer me anything to eat or drink. I would have to return to the Mess for all meals. I was shown the bathroom, but they added that as fuel for heating was rationed I could only have two baths a week.

Monsieur Kennis was a tall, lugubrious man, his wife small and timid. They both looked pale and under-nourished. They were not young and possibly were not too happy to have me billeted on them although they must have received some reimbursement for their trouble. I couldn't see myself spending much time in this house.

It was obvious the Belgian population had suffered greatly under the occupation. Everything was short. Coffee was unobtainable, many people ground up acorns as a substitute. Very soon I would become used to seeing old and young, rich and poor rummaging in the dustbins around our camp, looking for something to eat.

I made my way back to the Mess for dinner that evening. It was about a fifteen minute walk and I had to cut through the Butter Market. This was an ancient stone structure with a slate roof and a cobbled floor. As I crossed it, the sound of my heels echoed round the building.

At the Mess I found a much friendlier atmosphere. There was a large log fire and a long bar counter with an airman in attendance. I was welcomed with the popular local drink, an

Advocaat served in a glass with a long spoon in it. I was told that was the way it was drunk (or sipped) in Belgium.

We shared the Mess with several army officers from the Survey Regiment, a couple of Flight Lieutenants working in Intelligence, the Wing Commander and his assistant. We all sat round a large table in the dining room and started to get to know each other.

We had been warned not to expect meals of a high standard. It was not that the cook wasn't capable, but we were only allowed to eat canned fruit and vegetables. I could not understand why, as there was plenty of agricultural land around. Bob Huskisson, one of the Majors in the Survey Regiment explained 'It's because all crops grown here are fertilised with human excreta. It could be dangerous; we could pick up typhoid or perhaps dysentery.' I must say it shocked me. In the early days there, we were not able to drink tap water either as there was a possibility the Germans could have poisoned the source before leaving. We had to use bottled water when available, or otherwise beer.

After a relaxing evening, we were taken back to our billets by an Army driver in case we lost our way.

Next morning after breakfast the eight Filterers and the Sergeants crossed the road to the bank, which had been commandeered for use as our Operations Room. I never knew what happened to the bank staff. We set about planning the layout. There was already a direct line to Intelligence and to 11 Group Filter Room. We had a large table to work on; two slide rules, plenty of paper and pencils and not much else.

There would be two Sergeants on each watch and they would operate the two phones. The Filterers would work on the Radar information and the fall-of-shot position for each V2 as it was notified; extrapolate the curve back to the launch site, checking each other. There would be four watches coinciding with those in the Filter room.

We split up into four pairs. Peggy Jones was to work with me. I was delighted as she was responsible and quick and we got on well together. We became A Watch and were scheduled to start operations the following morning at 0800 hours. We spent the afternoon practicing our calculations on dummy runs of missile tracks until we felt confident.

After another pleasant evening in the Mess I returned to my billet. I was rather apprehensive because we had been told there were still a few Germans hiding in the town and we did not know whether they had been left as snipers. As I walked through the Butter Market I tried to make as little sound as possible. It was very dark and as there was still a curfew in operation there was no one about. I wished I had a companion. I wondered what Peter was doing.

Having been given a key to the house, I let myself in quietly. There was no sign of the owners, it was almost midnight and I guessed they had already gone to bed. I was never going to see much of them. From that day onwards they kept themselves to themselves and barely spoke. I spent as little time there as possible.

The following morning we put into practice what we had learned. About six V2s were launched during our watch. We extrapolated the curve each time successfully and calculated the position of the launch area, passing it on to Flight Officer Richmond. We were notified at the end of the watch that our calculations had resulted in two successful hits on the launchers by one of the Mosquito Sections. That made us feel great.

From then onwards this method coupled with the sound reports from the Survey Regiment was to prove a great success. Each day more and more launch vehicles were destroyed. The hope was that Hitler's factories would not be able to replace them before our troops advanced to their position.

During our second watch I managed to speak to Mary Hogg in the Filter Room and ask her to get a message to Peter to say I was fine and to write to me as soon as possible. It was over a week before I finally heard from him and he sounded very unhappy. I felt guilty since I was finding everything interesting and almost enjoyable. I was relieved when a second letter arrived to say he had been sent on a course to RAF St. Athan. I hoped that would take his mind off being parted.

I was finding plenty to do in any spare time I had. I had promised the Lizons, the Belgians I had met at Winchmore Hill, that I would call on their family in Brussels and tell them that they were being well-looked after in Britain and they were fine. Monsieur Lizon had asked whether I would deliver a parcel to them. A large packet arrived at the Mess in the first month. It caused a lot of consternation because it was not very securely packed and ground coffee was spilling out and perfuming the whole Mess.

I managed to find the family in the Brussels suburb of Grimberghen. The welcome I received was exceedingly friendly – not only because of the coffee I had brought but also because I could give them up-to-date news of their relatives in London. I was told that whenever I had time off, I could always spend it with them. This is a friendship that I have kept up even now.

Amongst the personnel of 33 Wing we found we had enough hockey players to form a team, a mixture of WAAF, RAF and

Army. Malines also had an excellent town team, all male, which had kept going throughout the occupation. The Conrad brothers were leading lights and lived only a few doors from the Mess. Several of us met them in a bar one night and they invited us to use their clubhouse and offered to play us.

On our first match there were four girls in our team and when the Malines team arrived we were shattered to find at least half of them were over six foot tall and also members of the Belgian national ice hockey team! We were fortunate to have Bob Huskisson on our side, a keen rugby player and all-round athlete – and although we girls were dwarfed by the men we were able to nip in and out and give the opponents a run for their money. I became great friends with the Conrads and would often spend time off duty in their house, where their parents gave me a great welcome.

Despite duty hours which were very concentrated and living conditions that were fairly bleak, we managed to have a good time when off duty as well as feeling we were doing something worthwhile. Night clubs were reopening in Brussels and often a group of us would spend an evening there. By now more and more airwomen had joined us, taking over some of the kitchen and admin duties from the men who were being moved on. We decided to make a club for them and the airmen.

We were given a ground floor flat that had been vacated by the Germans and did what we could to make a place for them to relax. Most of the girls were under twenty-five and had never been abroad before. They couldn't speak the language so we had a few problems with them feeling homesick. We were given permission to go to houses owned by collaborators who had been imprisoned, to borrow a few items to make the club more comfortable – chairs, a radio, and items for use in the kitchen. We always issued a receipt and told the families they could have them back when the war was over.

Two weeks before Christmas I was told I was being sent back to Britain for three days to choose some extra items to make the conditions better for the WAAF. I managed to let Peter know and he met me as the plane landed at Northolt. I had a lot to do, collecting as many items as possible ready for taking back to Belgium, but I managed to spend one afternoon and a night at *The Studio*.

It was then that Peter told me he had been so upset when I left that one day soon after, he had tried to smuggle himself into a plane going to Ghent. Of course he was found but, lucky for him, the Flight Lieutenant piloting the plane knew him and he was never reported. I tried to explain that it was necessary for me to be over there and we were doing something worthwhile. He said he understood but I wonder if he did.

During the short time I was back in Britain, I paid a brief visit to my parents' home. I was horrified to find the houses opposite had been destroyed by a V2. My mother had not told me, but our house had sustained considerable blast damage and she had been injured. 'Why didn't you tell me?' I asked.

'Well, I didn't want to worry you,' was her reply. I felt terrible to think she had been through that trauma and I had not supported her. It made me realise how much civilians had suffered, especially in London, and how their resilience contributed to the spirit that was Britain. A few years later when my mother died of terminal cancer, I wondered if the injuries she had received had contributed to this.

The return flight was crowded. I was sandwiched between a Major General, brother to Field Marshal Alexander, and the American crew of a Flying Fortress. Every seat was taken. Opposite me were two Military Police escorting two handcuffed civilians. It was whispered that they were spies. Heaped between the two long rows of seats was all the luggage. I had several large boxes of sports goods and books for the WAAF – there were kitbags, cases, trunks all piled on top of each other. The General was reading the News of the World and was indifferent to everyone and everything around him.

We were warned there was bad weather ahead and the flight might be a bit rocky! As we crossed the channel, we hit a violent snowstorm. The aircraft was buffeted; it would drop like a stone and then gradually climb again. Without seats belts, we were thrown about. The spies were the first to succumb. They were both sick over the luggage in front of me. The American pilots soon followed. I knew I would be next and just before it happened, I turned and grabbed the newspaper from the General and at least retained some dignity. We were almost ready to land. The airstrip was covered in ice and frozen snow and we slithered to a halt.

As we left the plane and breathed in the clean but icy air we quickly revived. The cargo of luggage was unloaded. Fortunately my boxes had survived the results of the turbulence. Before we were allowed to go into the airport building we were told that the plane had to return straight away. The only available runway was the Summerfield tracking, a heavy metal grid under the ice and snow on which we had landed, and we were all needed to help turn the plane around. This order included officers, as well as the General, and the one female aboard! So we lined up behind the wings and pushed. After a lot of heaving, we succeeded in our task. We were allowed to leave.

33 Wing had sent a Jeep to pick me up. I was delighted to see it was Bob Huskisson driving it and we quickly set out for Malines, about 80 kilometers away. It was still snowing heavily and the windscreen kept freezing up, so it was a slow and chilly drive back to base. We were both glad of a hot toddy when we reached the Mess. The WAAF were thrilled with the extra comforts I had managed to collect. Christmas was almost here.

Victory in Sight

From the middle of December weather conditions deteriorated dramatically. The temperature fell below freezing, fuel was short and everyone suffered from the cold. On December 17th, there was a heavy snowfall all over Belgium with strong winds and extensive low cloud. This halted all flying by the Allies.

The Germans took advantage of this and launched increasing numbers of V2s against Antwerp by day and night. Despite our efforts the launching lorries remained unchallenged.

On December 16th, Antwerp had suffered its greatest disaster. A V2 landed on the Rex Cinema in the centre of the city, killing over 500 people, most of them Allied troops. The authorities immediately shut all cinemas and theatres and decreed that no meetings could take place with more than 50 people. Antwerp became known as the *City of Sudden Death*.

Allied supply lines were becoming longer as our troops moved on towards the German border. It was vital to keep Antwerp open for supplies to get through. Each time we went on duty the pressure increased.

Meanwhile on the Russian front, German losses were increasing and it seemed the Soviets were planning a long winter campaign against ill-prepared enemy troops. Hitler and his Generals realised this and decided on a bold counter-attack, intended to reach Antwerp and split the British – already on their way to the Ruhr – from the Americans in the south. They hoped this would persuade the Allies to agree a peace in favour of the Axis powers.

This led to the von Rundstedt Offensive, Hitler's last gamble, which we know as the *Battle of the Bulge*. It was the largest and bloodiest battle the American forces fought throughout the war, resulting in 19,000 killed. The much smaller British forces involved lost 1,400 men.

This offensive was planned in complete secrecy by Hitler himself. He signed the order *Not to be altered*. Allied forces were no longer receiving Enigma intercepts since the Wehrmacht had dispensed with using radios for relaying orders. The battle front was shorter and they were now able to rely upon telephone and teleprinters for communication. The battle began on December 16th and raged unceasingly until late into January through the Ardennes forest to the borders of France and Luxembourg.

There were many initial successes for the Wehrmacht using their Panzer divisions. American troops were overcome and captured, and in some cases the prisoners of war were massacred. Bastogne was cut off after it was surrounded by the enemy. At 33 Wing, we were so busy with the increased number of V2 launches that we were unaware of the danger of our own position on the route to Antwerp.

By December 23rd the weather conditions improved and once more Allied air forces were able to operate, but it was not until January 25th that the battle was won and the German forces defeated. It was only then that we realised how near we had come to being overrun and captured or perhaps killed.

Meanwhile Christmas had come and gone. There was little time for festivities and no chance of an elaborate meal for either other ranks or officers. My only memory is of my surprise on one trip into Brussels at seeing the amazing innovative and beautiful window displays in the shops. I know the French are renowned for the artistry of their window-dressing but the shopkeepers of Brussels excelled them. Despite the shortage of food, fuel and any luxury goods, these displays were a welcome sight to the citizens.

I wondered what Peter would be doing for Christmas. He had written that he was now mostly involved in the camp entertainments. He had taken over the dance band from Bill Savill and was playing at various RAF stations around London. I was pleased he was busy. I was conscious of the difference in my work and his and wondered if he ever compared them.

Once the weather improved and the danger passed we were able to think about some leisure activities. With more personnel joining us we were able to raise two hockey teams. Our A and B teams regularly played each other, using the facilities of the local hockey club. The number of V2s increased during January as the Allies moved nearer to their bases, so any chance to relax in the fresh air was a welcome break.

The Conrads' timber business was the main source of wood to the numerous furniture manufacturers in Malines. The town had been famous for its furniture for many years. The family owned a sawmill in the Ardennes forest near the French border, where the recent fighting had been taking place. Unable to contact their workers during the battle, they were anxious to check up on how things were. Their son Pierre decided to drive there. He asked if I would like to join him and see more of the country. Since we were now having an easier workload, I was able to have a day off. I was delighted to have this opportunity, not realising then how near the battlefront we would be going.

One early morning during the second week in February Pierre arrived in a lorry. He explained he would be picking up a load of timber as they were almost out of stock. *'Cela ne te dérange pas – en camion?'* We usually talked in French. 'You don't mind – in a lorry?'

'Of course not.' I told him. I climbed into the right-hand seat of the cab and we set off. There was about eighty miles to go.

The weather was still cold but sunny. We stopped off at Namur for a coffee and then headed for Dinant and into the Ardennes forest. The snowfalls had been very deep in this area, where the Panzer divisions and the American tank regiments had fought only a short time before. As the temperature rose we could see the remains of the shattered tanks and far worse, the bodies of the fallen soldiers – both German and American – emerging from the melting snow. I shuddered as we passed ever more dead bodies. It was like a terrible dream; a massacre.

Pierre was relieved to find his sawmill undamaged and his workers unhurt but like me he was appalled at what must have been a fierce and bloody battle. He loaded a supply of timber and we moved on to Bouillon on the French border for a reviving coffee and a snack. Our journey back took us through Bastogne, which had been one of the major German targets. We returned to Malines that evening very subdued, realising how lucky we had been that the outcome of the Battle of the Bulge had been in our favour.

February gave way to March. V2 activity was decreasing as the Allies were nearing the launch sites. On March 18th I was called into Wing Commander Fry's office and told I was being sent to Paris to Supreme Headquarters Allied Expeditionary Force. I was to carry reports of the results obtained by 33 Wing and also give a personal report on the activities of the eight Filterers.

I was given a train warrant and I left on the 20th. I took a taxi from the Gare de l'Est. SHAEF was housed in the Palais de Versailles. I had visited there in 1937 and seen it in all its glory. Now I wondered how it had survived through the German occupation.

Reporting to the duty officer at Reception I was told I would be accommodated in *Les Petits Écuries* – the stables! I was assured I would be comfortable there and I would be eating in the main Officers' Mess.

The place was buzzing with activity and swarming with high-ranking officers from the Army, Navy and Air Force. As I walked round the building I was horrified to see the whole place denuded. No beautiful furniture, no tapestries on the walls, no pictures. Everything gone. This was the legacy of the Germans. Goering especially took every opportunity to ransack the treasures of the occupied countries. The damage was incalculable.

The meal that evening was a great deal better than anything I had eaten in the Mess at Malines or anywhere in Belgium. They had been able to call on the finest French chefs and procure the choicest French produce. The next few days were spent in interviews and reports to various departments interested in the techniques employed by 33 Wing. I got the feeling they were delighted with our efforts and the results achieved by the unit.

Finally, I had a spare day so I decided to go into Paris by Metro and see if I could find the hotel owned by the Boucher family, with whom I had stayed in the year before the war started. I hoped I might see those three children once more. They would be grown up by now, since they were only a few years younger than I was.

I headed for the Hotel de la Tremoille. It was only a stone's throw from the Place de la Concorde. As I entered the foyer it was immediately obvious that the hotel had been taken over by the American authorities. There was a US sergeant sitting at Reception. I asked to speak to the duty officer.

A Major appeared and shook my hand and was very pleasant. 'Hi there, what can I do for you?' he asked. I told him I was on an official visit to SHAEF but that I knew the Boucher family and I was hoping to see them. His reaction was immediate. He changed from welcoming mode to challenging in a second.

'Show me your papers,' he demanded, which of course I promptly did. He looked at them and calmed down a little and finally said: 'The best thing you can do is to forget them.' I asked why but he would say no more. 'There is nothing I can do for you here,' was all he would say. 'You had better leave.' I walked out of the hotel perplexed. If they had been killed he would have said. What could have happened?

It took me until the year 2000 to learn the truth. Alsace had been in the hands of the Germans until the end of World War One and there were still many close connections. Monsieur Boucher was a member of the French Parliament, the *Chambre des Députés*. During the occupation, he joined the Pétain government, a "*pétainiste*" supporting the Nazis. He was a collaborator.

In 1944, realising Germany was losing the war; he decided to save his skin. Sending his children on in advance, he and his wife escaped to Germany. They stayed there until 1946 and then to Italy, finally making their way to Spain, en route for the Argentine where he spent many years, dying in 1968. I learned that the Hotel de la Tremoille was later sold to the Grand Metropolitan Group, a British company. What happened to those children I do not know. Maybe they too are dead. I would like to find out.

Despite this unhappy incident there was one pleasant encounter in Paris. On a later day I looked up my brother's school pen-friend Roger Sirdey. I found him living at the address Dennis had given me. Roger was now twenty years old.

There was little chance of going to university during the occupation so he had found a job working at an ironmonger's shop. The owner was a leader of a Resistance cell and very soon Roger had joined the group. As he understood German he was given the job of delivery boy. The German garrison was near the shop and often used it for supplies. Roger would deliver these items on his bicycle. He was instructed to become friendly with the soldiers, listen to their conversation and report what he heard. There was a possibility of learning details of troop movements, delivery of new equipment or visits of important German Officers – anything that might be used by the Resistance fighters.

His family related all this over a family meal and a glass or two of wine. His efforts proved very useful but after the liberation they had unexpected repercussions. Collaborators at that time were immediately challenged by their neighbours and beaten up, even killed. People had seen Roger chatting to the Germans, apparently fraternising with the enemy. They were going to punish him as he turned up for work on the day of liberation. Roger only escaped injury when his boss came out just in time and assured them that he was a member of the Resistance.

When I left, Roger gave me a book called *Paris sous la Botte des Nazis* – Paris under the Boot of the Nazis. It contained pictures taken secretly by the members of the Resistance showing many of the awful things that had happened during those years. There were very few printed. It is a book I treasure.

That Paris trip was momentous. Two contacts– one a collaborator, one a Resistance fighter. Returning to Malines I mused on how my life and the lives of so many people I knew had changed since those days of peace.

Beginning of the End

I arrived back at Malines on March 24th. It was noticeable that the number of both V1s and V2s being tracked had reduced dramatically. The V2 we tracked the following day was the last one to fall on Antwerp and the final V1 fell two days later. The Allied forces had crossed into Germany and occupied the firing sites. We were not to know this and continued to operate as usual. Lord Haw-Haw had been warning for some weeks that there was a third weapon of vengeance ready to attack, the V3. We were expecting this to arrive daily.

Despite being only 12 kilometers from Antwerp, Malines had been lucky. A couple of missiles had fallen on the outskirts of the town but done little damage. One V2 had fallen in the centre but failed to explode and had been placed outside the bank where we worked. Each day as we entered the building, we would pass it and wonder.

Antwerp on the other hand had suffered terribly. 1,736 people had been killed and 4,500 injured. Damage to the city's buildings and homes was enormous. It would take years to repair. The people of the city had suffered six months of terror. But at last it seemed they were no longer under attack.

The port, although constantly damaged, had managed to effect swift repairs and the unloading of troops and supplies had continued as the Allies pushed forward. However, the expected

214

amount of supplies was curtailed by the V2 attacks and the Allies had been forced to fly men and ammunition to Ghent. The V2 campaign overall had some effect, not perhaps as much as Hitler had thought. Because we had finally destroyed all his launching vehicles, this had reduced and eventually stopped the attacks.

On March 28th Mussolini, who had escaped from prison, was found by members of an Italian anti-fascist group in a part of Italy not yet occupied by the Allied forces. He was summarily executed and his body taken to Milan and hung there to prove his demise. By the end of April, Germany's vital Ruhr manufacturing area was captured and Hanover fell the following day.

We continued to cover the twenty-four hour watches but with only one Filterer and one sergeant on duty during the daytime. We were then free to take on other duties. In order to help the local authorities throughout Belgium to restore services, rebuild schools and hospitals, the Allies appointed a Town Major, usually an army officer, in each town, to work with the Mayor. Several of us were seconded to help with office duties. I worked on several occasions with the Town Major's team and got to know them well. The work they did helped Belgium to get on its feet again.

It was obvious that Germany was finished. Most of Berlin was in Russian hands. Hitler, fearing he might suffer the same fate as Mussolini, committed suicide on April 30th. General Wolff, Commander of the Wehrmacht, signed a surrender document ending the Battle of Berlin on May 2nd. By the 7th all German forces had surrendered.

Sergeant Halstead and I took over the midnight watch on the night of the 7th/8th May. Although much of this news had not reached us, we realised the end of war in Europe was imminent. ,

Now there was little activity. As I left the bank at the end of the night watch, a few minutes after the sergeant, a small black car pulled to a sudden screeching halt in front of me. The door opened and a pilot jumped out and grabbed hold of my arm. 'Am I glad to see you! You're the first English girl we've seen since 1940!' It was then I noticed chalked on the side of the car – *Ex-POWS!*

They were two Wellington bomber pilots who had been shot down during a bombing mission in September 1940 and had been in a prisoner of war camp north of Hanover ever since. They told me they had been driving during the night hours for the last few days, hoping to evade capture. Most of the guards had deserted the camp some days earlier, realising the Allies were approaching.

The two airmen had seized the opportunity to steal a German army vehicle and escape. Eventually they had reached a liberated part of Holland and cadged some petrol from a farmer. It was then they decided to write the sign on the car so they were not mistaken for Germans. They were overjoyed to find a British person after their hazardous journey.

I took them over to the Mess to meet the Wing Commander. We gave them an enormous breakfast since they had been existing on what they could forage. The CO asked them what they would like to do. At that moment the official news came through that Germany had surrendered unconditionally. The war in Europe was over. It was VE day! The whole Mess broke into cheers; we all hugged and kissed each other. We were laughing and crying.

The two pilots turned to Wing Commander Fry and said: 'We want to go back to Rotterdam and find the nurses who saved our lives after we crashed. Any chance of taking some food to them?'

The CO turned to me: 'You'd better go with them and take someone else with you. They'll be bomb-happy at being free so keep your eye on them!'

I asked Peggy Jones to join us. 'You bet,' she said.

An hour later we set off in the German car with a box filled with cans of corned beef, tins of jam, biscuits and a bag of coffee. Rotterdam was about 70 miles away. The two pilots were singing away and in high spirits. I tried to imagine how terrible it must have been to be a prisoner of the Germans for five years.

As we entered Holland everyone was celebrating the news. It had been one of the last occupied countries to be freed. The journey took us through small towns and country villages. The roads were full of farm wagons piled high with branches of gorse – the golden flower symbolising the Dutch Monarchy, the House of Orange.

We finally reached the bank of the Rhine only to find, to our great disappointment that all the bridges had been destroyed. We looked around to see if there was any way of crossing the river. We could see Rotterdam on the other side. Finally we found a small ferry boat. We asked the skipper to take us across, explaining the reason, but to our dismay he refused. He told us the river been mined by the retreating Germans. He was able to go alone in his small boat to pick up a few supplies for the village, but with us in it too, it would be too dangerous.

We talked together and decided the only thing was to give him the name of the nurses and the hospital and ask him to deliver the box. He promised he would do this. There was no alternative, but I often wonder whether those nurses received it. Holland had been the scene of recent fighting, food was short. The temptation must have been very strong for the ferryman to keep the food or sell it for a handsome profit.

We returned to the Mess by early evening. The airmen were on a high but I was feeling tired, having been up for nearly thirty hours. The Medical Officer saw me and said: 'You look as if you should be in bed.' I told him I was too excited to sleep. 'Take this,' he said and handed me a couple of sleeping tablets.

I walked back to the Kennis house, took one of the tablets and undressed. As I climbed into bed, it hit me. This was Victory Night! What on earth was I doing? I couldn't miss this. It was history!

I jumped up, had a quick wash, put on a clean shirt and my best uniform and rushed back to the Mess. Just in time. Everyone was preparing to go to Brussels. The MO saw me and said: 'So you changed your mind. Hang on; I'll give you something to keep you going!' He dived into his bag and produced a Benzedrine. I had never taken drugs of any sort but here was I, having first *a downer and then an upper!*

I climbed into the pilots' commandeered car with three others and joined the rest on the road to the Belgian capital. The people of Brussels were delirious with happiness. They lined the streets shouting and cheering as we joined the procession of cars and jeeps and trucks, full of British and American service personnel.

The euphoria was contagious. People threw flowers as we passed, offered us bottles of wine, cakes, anything they could find to say thank you. It was a magical time. At first I was quite sleepy but as the Benzedrine kicked in, I ended up singing and dancing with the rest. Dawn was breaking as we headed back to Malines.

A night to remember! As I finally went to sleep in the early hours, I wondered how Peter had spent his Victory night.

I woke up in time for a late lunch in the Mess. The two pilots, Bob and Joe, were still there, I never did learn their surnames. They would stay another night with us and then they left to report to HQ 2nd Tactical Air Force to be flown home.

We shut down all operations in the bank and transferred the phone connections to the main office. We were given a couple of days off before they decided how best to use us. We were told we would not be going home yet, there was still work to be done. I sent a letter to Peter telling him the news. I was sure he expected me back almost immediately.

I decided to spend my time off trying to find two young Belgians, brother and sister, Pierre and Andrée, whom I had met before the war when my parents took Dennis and me to Ostend for a week's holiday. We became friends on the roller-skating rink and we had corresponded up until the war. I looked for their surname Serruys in the telephone directory. There were just two. I hit the target with the first call and spoke to their mother whom I'd also met. She immediately invited me to come and visit them. They would meet me at the railway station. I recognised them at once.

We walked to their mother's house where they told me their story over a glass of wine. Andrée, who very tall and good-looking, was married and had a little girl. Pierre, equally handsome, worked for the government and lived at home. Sadly their father had been shot when foraging for food after the curfew. But it was the mother's story which intrigued me.

She had been a member of the Belgian Resistance and kept a safe house for airmen who had been shot down but rescued by the Resistance before being captured. They would stay with her for a few days and then be moved at night on to the next stage of their journey to freedom.

She had some interesting tales to tell but the only one I can now remember was how an airman would be hidden in an empty beer barrel and rolled down a hill to a lorry waiting to take him on the next part of his journey. There must be many such untold tales of how ordinary civilians in the occupied countries did their bit to help. All too soon it was time for me to return to Malines but I promised another visit as soon as possible.

After all the busy and exciting months of work, the next few days were spent in completing extensive reports on our contribution to Operation Crossbow at 33 Wing, 2nd TAF. A week later we would be allocated our future duties.

Breendonk:
Camp of Silence and Death

There was much speculation amongst all of us at 33 Wing as to how we would be deployed, where we would be sent and what we would do. Already many RAF personnel from units in Belgium had returned to Britain for reposting, perhaps to the Far East. In the meantime Belgium needed help to regain peacetime stability.

In the days following VE Day, 33 Wing was gradually closing down, our job done. Some airwomen and a few Filterer Officers had already been sent back to Fighter Command for duties there. Those who had joined the WAAF earliest would now receive training towards helping them back to civilian life and would be the first demobilised. The rest of us were given various admin duties – compiling records, arranging postings or working with the Town Major's department.

I was anxious to know what my fate would be. When I was told what I was to do, it came as a total surprise and a considerable shock. Exactly a week after VE Day I was called into the C.O's office and told that as I was able to converse adequately in French, I was to act as a guide and interpreter. For what? To where?

Only twelve kilometres from Malines near a town called Willebroek was a fortress. It had been built in 1909 on an original Roman site, as part of the fortifications encircling Antwerp in preparation for any German attack. At the beginning of World War Two it was used as an office for King Leopold, but when the German army invaded neutral Belgium in 1940 they had taken it over for a much more sinister purpose.

At first it was used as a holding camp for Belgian Jews, prior to their being transported in railway wagons from Malines to Auschwitz. A particularly cruel and vicious SS officer, Lager Commandant Philipp Schmitt, took over and changed it into a concentration camp not only for Jews but homosexuals, gypsies and above all, captured Resistance fighters. Treatment there became harsher, more stringent, and much crueller.

Some Belgian youths formed their own SS. Many of these men were employed there and put in positions of authority over their fellow countrymen. Fort Breendonk became notorious and greatly feared. Despite being a small camp, many people considered it as terrible a place as Auschwitz or Bergen-Belsen.

There was one guard for every ten prisoners. Few were ever freed. Nearly 500 died there, many from starvation. The rest perished after being sent to the other death camps. In August 1944, as the Allies made their way through France, the Germans closed the camp and the remaining prisoners were despatched to Auschwitz. This Belgian hellhole was where I was being sent.

The local RAF commander in Belgium decided that as many personnel as possible should be shown this camp and learn of the terrible events that had taken place within its walls. My grim task was to escort these groups each day and tell them what had taken place there. And so it began – an experience I had never expected to undergo and the beginning of memories that have stayed with me to this very day.

On the first morning the RAF driver picked me up at the Mess at 0815 hours. We drove for about half an hour through pleasant countryside and villages to the small town of Willebroek. I sat silently wondering what I would encounter. Fort Breendonk lay on the outskirts.

As we approached I could see high earth mounds concealing the camp. The driver dropped me there. I told him to return three hours later. I turned and walked over the stone bridge to the front entrance. I saw the whole site was surrounded by a wide moat, filled with murky water. My heart was beating rapidly; I could already feel the menace of the place.

Entering the archway I was stopped by a guard. I showed him my letter of introduction and my RAF pass and he fetched the Head Warder, a man in his mid-forties. He told me he had been expecting me. We spoke in French, although I imagined from his accent that he normally spoke Flemish. He explained that prior to the war he had been in the prison service. He had joined the Resistance during the occupation and fortunately was never discovered.

We crossed the main courtyard. It was filled with prisoners, men mostly in their late teens and their twenties. They stared at me with what I took to be animosity. The prison officer took me on a tour of the camp, explaining the main points of interest – and cruelty. He said that when I was taking the airmen around, he would be with me in case they wished for any further information. He seemed amiable enough although he showed little expression.

As we began the tour my first question was: 'Who are the men exercising in the courtyard?' He explained that they were Belgian collaborators who had actively helped the Germans during the occupation. Many had joined the Belgian SS and had worked as guards in the camp. They had been as vicious as their paymasters. They would go on trial very soon and many of them would pay the penalty of their treason with execution.

As the tour round the prison camp continued, the stories I was told chilled my blood. Initially it was used to round up Belgian Jews before they were transported by cattle truck from the holding station at Malines. They lived in concrete bunkers that had no heating. Their sleeping quarters, designed for 30, were accommodating double that number. The bunks were three-tiered and they slept on straw mattresses. In the daytime their toilet facilities consisted of two trenches in the main courtyard. They were only allowed to stay there two minutes, otherwise they were beaten. I could imagine the consequences.

Food for the Jews was less than for other prisoners and many died of starvation. During the years of the German occupation, more and more members of the Resistance would be imprisoned there, especially the Communists. In order to make them talk, they would first be put in solitary confinement cells. The ceilings of these cells were open grilles, giving them a cage-like appearance. Some of the prisoners would be manacled, with their hands secured above their heads to the wall, and their feet chained. They had two meals a day served through a cat-hole in the door. In order to eat, their hands would be freed but they had to lie on the floor to reach the food, like animals. Those destined for special punishment were softened up with the harshest treatment.

BREENDONK: CAMP OF SILENCE AND DEATH

As I entered these cells I saw how some had scratched messages on the walls with their fingernails. One Resistance fighter had written: *Trahi par ma maitresse, Leonardine Boissons de Courtrai.* Betrayed by my mistress, Leonardine Boissons from Courtrai. One inmate had drawn the face of Christ, another had marked the days of his imprisonment in the cells by scratched lines in rows of seven.

The most horrifying place of all was the torture chamber, a large bare room with high ceilings and no windows. The only things in the room were a large stand bearing a butcher's block on it, scarred and stained, and a small wooden slatted bed. The warder told me that as well as beating the prisoners and torturing them with hot irons, electric current would be applied to all the orifices of the body to induce them to talk, to betray their comrades. When they collapsed or fainted, they were thrown on the bed and the jack-booted guards would stamp on their legs to bring them round. The broken slats bore witness to the force used and the many broken bones suffered.

To let the next poor creature destined for this treatment know what was to happen to him, he was made to stand behind a short partition and hear the cries of anguish of the one being tortured.

Outside in a hidden corner I saw the gallows and nearby the posts stained brown with blood where the executions took place. In another area was a huge empty piece of tilled ground. Here Jews would be buried up to their necks, often suffocating. Over four thousand captives were incarcerated in this camp during those dreadful years. Several hundreds died here. Many more were brutally tortured before being sent to their death in other concentration camps. Those not tortured were subjected to forced labour, building the huge earth wall surrounding the camp and

225

hiding it from view. They had the minimum of tools and sometimes had to dig with their bare hands.

Very few prisoners were ever released but I was to meet one of those lucky few, a man who lived locally and had been incarcerated as a homosexual. He told me how those already ill were encouraged to die. They were sent to the bath area, stripped of their clothes and made to wait in the open air whatever the weather, then plunged into baths of scalding water. After emerging, once more they had to stand naked for a further time outside. Many died of pneumonia within a few days. He described how he had been tied with others to a large wheel and for hours had to push it round to draw water from the well. He had a comparatively easy time.

After that first visit I returned to my waiting transport emotionally drained. I was unable to talk about it for the whole of the return journey even though the driver asked me. For the next two weeks I continued to take parties of RAF personnel, about ten at a time, and show them of the horrors of Breendonk. Many were already hardened by war but had tears in their eyes as they listened.

I had to steel myself daily to relate these horrors. Until they saw the torture chamber and heard the warder's descriptions, many said they could not have believed that so-called civilised people could think up such atrocities. And every day as we walked through the courtyard, the Belgian traitors exercising there would swear at us in Flemish and even urinate at me. I would walk past and hold my head high and tell the airmen these men had betrayed their friends and their country.

The memories of those two weeks will never leave me. Often at night, I awaken and see again those messages scratched with bloodied nails, by the doomed prisoners on the walls of the cells. There are still many people who will never forget the horrors of Auschwitz, Bergen-Belsen and Treblinka. I will never forget Fort Breendonk.

Picking up the Threads

Returning to normal admin duties at 33 Wing gave me a strange feeling – I felt as though all the horrors of Breendonk were just a dream. Peggy Jones noticed I was very quiet and asked: 'What happened to you?' I found myself pouring out what I'd seen and what I'd heard. She could hardly believe it.

'Did they have any idea when they sent you there what it would be like?' she asked.

'I don't think so,' I replied.

'Well, they had no right to put you through that.' I tried to explain that someone had to let us Brits know what so-called civilised people are capable of doing and perhaps realise what we had been fighting for and fighting against.

I was called into the Wing Co's office to report and he was equally surprised. 'Still, you coped,' he said.

Most of the Filter Room personnel were preparing to return to Fighter Command Headquarters for re-mustering – allocation to other duties. Peggy Jones was going back to Canada so I realised I probably would not see her again. I would miss her, she had been a great companion and we had worked well together. The Army Survey Regiment officers had already returned to the UK. There were only a few of us left.

They'd had an easy time during my absence – better food, time to explore the countryside and some of the nearby towns,

228

PICKING UP THE THREADS

and plenty of trips to Brussels. On my first night back Flight Lieutenant Harris returned from Lille with a special treat for us. We were having a drink in the Mess bar when he arrived carrying a large sack. He tipped it out on the counter – surprise, surprise, it was a pile of oysters. There and then he started opening them and passed round a couple of lemons he had also found to squeeze on them. We ate them from the shells, delicious. It was a far cry from Breendonk but I needed to wipe those images from my mind, at least for a while.

A couple of days later we were given the date when 33 Wing would close down. Everyone would be returning to their home bases by June 8th. Still unable to telephone Peter I sent a letter, hoping it would arrive before I did. Before I finally said au revoir to Belgium I had one last pleasant surprise. The Mayor of Malines gave a banquet to thank the Town Major and those who had worked with him for their help in restoring vital roads, bridges and services destroyed as the German occupiers retreated. I was invited as a guest.

It was an experience I have never matched before or since – a banquet lasting four hours and consisting of eight courses, starting with a *Vin d'Honneur* at 2000 hours and finishing at 0200 the following morning. In between each course someone gave a speech – some in French, some in Flemish and the final one in English by the Town Major.

Belgium is not as renowned as France for its gastronomy but on this occasion the chefs excelled themselves. During my time there, eating out occasionally in Brussels, I had remarked on their skill in producing great meals out of their restricted supplies. This banquet was of the highest standard yet. I love the way the continentals make eating a special occasion, without hurrying

229

and with pauses for conversation. This occasion was a fitting way to say goodbye.

Before our departure I managed a farewell visit to Andrée and Pierre Serruys and the Lizon family and a special goodbye to the Conrads, who had been exceedingly kind to all the Officers, opening their home to us. Would I ever see any of them again?

Back to Ghent airstrip, a short flight to Northolt and we were back at Stanmore, arriving on a beautiful sunny July day. No sign of Peter as we landed so I guessed perhaps he hadn't received my letter yet. This time there was a bedroom available in Bentley Manor, No.2 WAAF Officers' Mess. Most of my previous colleagues had gone – some pregnant and demobbed, and others already posted away for other duties.

As soon as possible I got a message through to Peter and told him I was home. He was surprised; my letter had not yet arrived. He said he would ask for a forty-eight hour pass for the end of the week and perhaps even get a few hours off the following day. He sounded delighted.

I was more apprehensive – it had been months since I had seen him during my short trip before Christmas. He was a stranger. I knew so little about him. What would we do after our demob? What work would he get? I knew the flat was ready for us but I couldn't sit there all day and do nothing, I would have to find something to occupy me. But now I was still in the Air Force and would be for a while.

It was not until four days later that Peter and I met up again. I was able to spend each night with him. The first evening we had supper with his parents. There was no food in the flat and no refrigerator. He was obviously happy I was home. He knew he would not be demobbed before March or April of the following year but had been told he would remain at Northolt until then. I suggested perhaps it would be a good idea if I volunteered to stay on. At least it would be two lots of pay coming in and I could apply to "live out" as the flat was only a few hundred yards from Command Headquarters.

I realised it would all depend on what work I was to do and where. It was two weeks before I received my orders. Once more I was surprised. Not admin, thank goodness. I was to go on an EVT course. 'What's that?' I asked.

'Educational and Vocational Training.' was the reply. It was a month's course where I would learn how to teach – part practice and part psychological training.

It meant going to a camp near Preston. I was told to take seven days leave. Immediately I contacted Peter to see if he could get leave at the same time. 'I'll do all I can. They know you've been away for so long, so maybe I'll get it.' He sounded pleased. He was not so happy to learn I would be going away again for another four weeks, but he returned the following day with a seven day pass.

We began to get to know each better. We went out on several days on his motor bike, the first time I had ever been on a pillion seat. We visited the places he had known as he was growing up. It was obvious he preferred the country to town living. We bought a few things for the flat including a fridge and I cooked my first meal for him. We got on well and laughed and talked about everything under the sun. We slept together for the longest time since we were married nearly a year ago. I realised he was very kind and considerate. I hoped I deserved him

The week flew by. Peter returned to Northolt and the following morning I reported to the duty officer that I would be prepared to stay on after my demob date. I knew they were going to need WAAF officers as so many had now left. On July 29th I took the train to Preston.

Learning to Teach

Lancashire once more, but this time somehow it was different. Perhaps because the war was over I now found the friendliness I had expected on my previous visit. People were smiling, welcoming.

The EVT courses were taking place in a mansion outside the town. We were accommodated in various buildings in the grounds. As we met for the opening lecture I found my fellow students were a mixed bag; WAAF and RAF officers from aircrew to medics, admin to signals, Section Officer to Wing Commander. There were non-commissioned officers, both WAAF and RAF, again from all branches and all commands – Bomber, Fighter, Maintenance and Coastal.

We were brought together to learn how to pass on any skills or knowledge we possessed to RAF and WAAF personnel of all ranks. The intention was to prepare them for re-entry into civilian life, giving them confidence and perhaps another tool to help them on their way. It was a bold concept – but would we learn enough in four weeks to be successful? I could see it was going to be a challenge.

The instructors came from all walks of life. There were academics, teachers, qualified engineers and time-serving craftsmen. As the days went by we were taught and tested. We learnt the psychology of teaching, the stance, the approach and

233

the techniques. We were shown how to demonstrate, how to use a blackboard, how to keep a student's interest. I found it both fascinating and ingenious. Much of the knowledge I acquired in those four weeks has been of use to me in the years since.

But I had a problem. The first morning as I took a shower I was sick, the second morning I was sick, the third morning I was sick again. I guessed I was pregnant. John a bomber pilot, already twice a father, recognised the signs from my rather jaundiced face as I entered the classroom and the occasional hasty retreat to the ablutions. One morning as we left for the morning session, he said: 'You're pregnant, aren't you?'

'I think I am. In fact I'm almost sure.'

'You are,' he assured me. 'Let me carry your case.' He looked after me like an elder brother and helped me through those first ten days. Then the symptoms stopped and all was normal. But yes, he was right. I was pregnant. I will never forget his help. I have no idea where he went at the end of the course, where his home was, what happened to him. We were again ships that passed in the night – he was a welcome one.

We would often spend the evenings in a local bar discussing the day's lessons and wondering what and who we would be asked to teach on our return to our units and when we would be demobbed. On August 18th we learned Japan had finally surrendered, it was VJ Day and we spent the evening celebrating, all ranks together in our favourite bar. We realised that at last the war was over. Maybe we would all be going home soon. It was an evening to remember.

As the course came to an end, each in turn had to take a class in a subject of their choice and give a demonstration on that theme. None of us knew exactly who or what we would teach when we returned to our stations but it seemed to stimulate us all. I certainly had no idea who my students would be, but I assumed they would be WAAF. So when it was my time to give a class I decided to talk about the use of herbs in cooking.

We were encouraged to find different methods to illustrate the lesson, rather than only write on the blackboard. Several of us went into Preston to get ideas. I found a fancy goods shop and unearthed a couple of tea towels with drawings of herbs on them, as I couldn't find any of the real thing. I built my lesson around these.

One of the corporals who was a car mechanic borrowed a book from a garage and taught on car maintenance. The bomber pilot called John who had taken me under his wing talked about model-making, his pre-war passion. As long as we could hold the interest of the class, we passed muster. What we would finally teach remained to be seen. As far as I know, we all passed and were given a certificate to that effect! But I had some special news to tell Peter.

Back at Stanmore I rang him at once. 'We're going to have a baby!' He was thrilled, but I told him I was not going to tell the Medical Officer yet. I thought I could stay in the WAAF as long as I felt fit to cope. It would be the end of March or early April 1946 before Peter's demob number would come up, and besides we needed the money.

It was now time to find out who and what I was going to teach. To my amazement, I was told that as I spoke a couple of foreign languages, I was to give classes to Polish air crew from fighter squadrons to help them improve their English. Most of them had escaped to Britain from their homeland at the outbreak of war when the Germans took over their country. After six years their limited vocabulary was peppered with RAF slang – *wizard prang, going for a burton, pukka job, bang on, shooting a line, u/s, dicey!* We could understand them, but would the general public?

The Russians had now taken control of Poland and put in a puppet government. One of the old school of politicians had suffered a sinister fatal accident, reported to have fallen from a high window in an official building. These Polish airmen were anxious, realising that there would be little future for them under the Soviet regime, even if they were allowed to return. They had decided to make their home in Britain in the hope that their families eventually might be able to join them. They needed to learn the language properly. It was up to me to help improve their accent, increase their vocabulary and give them the confidence to integrate in post-war Britain. I hoped I was up to it.

I was allocated a small room in the headquarters building at Bentley Priory and given a portable blackboard, a box of chalk, some English dictionaries and a pile of notebooks. The rest was up to me. They would have a class lasting two hours each weekday morning and another during the afternoon. As our flat over the stables was so close, I was permitted to live there.

I looked forward to this change. It was certainly going to be less onerous than filtering on an eight-hour watch, working under great pressure. Peter too was pleased with this arrangement as he could get home by motor bike frequently now. He too was giving physical training instruction to the airmen at Northolt, hoping to get them fit for civilian life, as well as playing occasional dance band engagements at units nearby.

The following Monday morning I met my first class of pupils. I was intrigued to find them mostly high-ranking officers. There was one Flight Lieutenant and the remainder ranged from

Squadron Leader to the most senior, Group Captain Bajn. There were eighteen in all. They were eager to make the most of the opportunity to perfect their English.

No one had taught me how to teach English so I had to work it out for myself. After talking to them I decided their accent was the first thing to concentrate on and gradually I would add more words to their repertoire. Later I could introduce grammar as I saw how they improved. But how could I explain the sounds of our language?

Pre-war I had learnt Pitman's shorthand, which is based on symbols for all the different sounds: the short and long vowels *á é í ó ú, ay ee iy oh yoo*, and the consonants, plus the joint sound of *th, sh, ch and wh*. So I evolved a way of getting them used to all these sounds and repeating them over and over again. Then I would read aloud a piece of good but simple prose and get them in turn to read it, following my accent and accentuation as closely as possible. We would have a lot of laughs on the way.

As they improved we would talk about everyday things. We would do a mock-up of shopping for food and for clothes. They would learn how to address people and talk about the weather. Slowly their vocabulary and accent improved, with less RAF slang. And it was fun!

As their confidence grew they talked of their families, usually with great emotion. They would tell me how they had escaped to join the British forces. They each had a tale to tell. They were a great bunch of men. I already knew that the Polish fighter pilots had the reputation for the highest success rate in bringing down the enemy bombers.

Group Captain Bajn, who was by far the oldest of them, had flown in the First World War when he had lost his right hand. I had wondered why he always wore a glove. Despite having a prosthetic replacement he had flown many missions in this war and had many "kills". My admiration for all of them grew daily.

No. 2 WAAF Mess was very different now. Many of the girls I had spent so much time with had gone. Grog was one of the first to return to civilian life as she had joined up in September 1939. Mary Hogg, now married to a fighter pilot, was also a civilian once more. Zoe Hicks too. My special friend "Willi", Section Officer Williams, had been sent to set up a new Filter Room in Colombo, Sri Lanka – then called Ceylon very soon after I had arrived in Belgium. She had then been appointed Personal Assistant to Air Vice Marshal Goddard and escorted him into the then French Indo-China as the Japanese retreated. She had not yet returned to Britain. However, we were to keep in touch until she died a few years ago.

It was sad to think that after all the busy and sometimes traumatic watches we had shared together I had not been able to say goodbye. At least Vera Everatt, although posted, has remained a good friend ever since. Sadly she and Grog have both been diagnosed with Dry Macular Degeneration of the eyes. They are now in their nineties and almost blind. I too have been diagnosed with a form of the same disease and have constant treatment to retain my sight. I wonder if all those years we spent working underground with inefficient lighting contributed to this condition. We will never know.

Meanwhile I was growing plumper! Finally, early in December, I reported to the Medical Officer, who declared I was almost five months pregnant. She asked me: 'Didn't you realise?' I pleaded ignorance. It was time to leave the WAAF under Clause 22, diagnosis of pregnancy. I was demobbed two days before Christmas 1945 and given the princely sum of £100 gratuity and the right to retain my rank. I spent Christmas Day as a civilian and a potential mother with Peter, who had the day off, and his family. I visited my parents for my first free Boxing Day for five years.

Coming to Terms

The shock of being a commissioned officer in His Majesty's Forces one day and just another pregnant woman the next was difficult to handle, that feeling of belonging to a team of dedicated people no longer there. I spent those first few days of the New Year feeling lost, bewildered. My identity had gone.

I was lonely. Peter was only home on the occasional night. My new in-laws were still strangers and very busy people. They had one of the most renowned riding schools in Britain to run. There were more than forty horses to look after, some kept at livery for private owners, some their own. There were five rides daily and dressage practice, a huge indoor school to maintain, two stable blocks, 10 loose boxes and 30 acres of farmland for the horses living out. With four stable hands to supervise and six resident students studying for the Institute of the Horse examination, they had no time to bother with me, sitting in the flat above the stables. It wasn't that they didn't care but their days were always full. Looking after animals is a twenty-four hour job.

Almost six months pregnant I still felt fit so I walked a lot, frequently over Stanmore Common. I would pass the entrance to RAF Bentley Priory and wonder what was going on behind the guarded gates. As I did not drive – too young to learn before the war and with no opportunity since – I felt imprisoned. As I walked, I realised it was up to me to do something to give my life a meaning.

I knew that my mother-in-law Tommie, although untrained, did all the office work, the correspondence and the accounts, as well as looking after the students and organising the daily rides. I had all the skills to help – shorthand, typing, book-keeping. So I approached Captain Younghusband, Jimmy, and asked if they would like some assistance.

He was delighted. He had had a serious brain operation early in the war and found any form of paperwork a strain. But he loved teaching and also his work with the film studios, providing horses and coaches for many of the new films now being made and training the stars to ride. Tommy was not so keen to hand over the reins, although she had enough to do, looking after the resident students, collecting the fees from the riders and the owners of horses at livery.

Jimmy suggested I took over the accounts and any of the necessary correspondence. It took up about two hours a day and it helped to integrate me into the family. I began to meet the clients and would join the riders for coffee after the prestigious Sunday ride when all the city businessmen came for their weekly exercise with Jimmy, hacking over the Common. Tommie was still a little put out that I had taken over the Riding School accounts so each day she would copy my entries into her own set of books and regard herself as in charge. But it didn't bother me and it kept her happy, and she was a very generous woman who was always showering us with gifts.

Two weeks later I found another call on my time. The RAF asked whether I would consider resuming my English lessons as the Polish officers were missing them and were due to be demobbed in a few weeks. 'Of course.' I replied, 'They can come here whenever they like.' And so it was.

They would turn up in the flat and over coffee we would continue practising. This time it was just conversation. They were doing well and feeling confident to face their new life as British residents. To my delight, the RAF informed me I would be paid twenty-eight shillings an hour (£1.40p). This added up to more than my Section Officer's pay a month. Civilian life looked a little more appealing.

I was able to invest in extra things for the baby. I had always liked the prams that the Belgians had, not as huge and unwieldy as the ones in Britain. Peter managed to persuade Squadron Leader Walker to buy one on his next flight to Ghent.

I continued to teach my Polish friends until the middle of March, when they arrived one day with a bottle of Polish vodka to say goodbye. Their demob date had arrived and they were leaving the following morning. We had a farewell toast and they presented me with a book, entitled *Poland's Progress*, relating the changes in their country from 1919 to 1939 when the Germans took over. It was signed by them all, such wonderfully exotic names – Philipowicz, Novak, Havitz, Tzsykowski, Sponarowitz and of course Bajn, with some I could not decipher. Brave men, every one.

It was March 23rd when the pains started. My mother-in-law drove me down to the private nursing home, situated in Prime Minister Atlee's former home. It was run by one of the riding school's clients, Dr. Eleanor Bergmann. She had escaped from Austria at the time of the Anschluss and now had a thriving business.

I had no say in the matter. These were the days when pregnant mums had no checks beforehand, no ultrasound pictures. You just hoped for the best. I was four days in the first stage of labour with nothing for the pain. You had to grin and bear it! Finally at two o'clock on the fifth morning it was all over and I had a healthy new baby weighing six and a half pounds.

Peter was still at Northolt but due to be demobbed the following day. He managed to get home that night to see his new son. Then he had to return at once to hand in his kit and go through the motions to become plain Mister again. After six and a half years' service, most of the time as a Corporal, he returned home with a £32 gratuity and an ill-fitting demob suit. Five days later the baby and I left the nursing home in Peter's new acquisition, a Morgan three-wheeler. The metamorphosis from Filterer Officer to mother was complete.

Was it easy? No, my maternal instincts were not highly developed but I soon learnt. My mother and father came to inspect. My brother Dennis had by now been called up for his two years of National Service. He too was in the Air Force, his university studies put on hold. They trained him as an electrician – very useful for household repairs – and from this humble start he went on to become a PhD specialising in Physics and Bio-medical engineering, finally moving to the USA and working for NASA.

Our son was baptised Clive Francis Younghusband. I loved him dearly but I found that after nearly six years, coping with the challenges of war and the responsibilities I had assumed from the age of nineteen, I needed more than just domesticity in my life. I wondered whether I would ever find anything to fill this need.

Many of my WAAF friends also found it difficult to adjust. I maintained regular contact with "Willi," "Grog" and Vera Everatt. Several others stayed in touch for a while. Some had happy marriages and were content, other marriages collapsed.

Some never found a mate. One who shall be nameless died of alcoholism, unable to face life in a country village with little going on after having been one of our most successful Filter Officers. One sadly committed suicide. I wonder if today's generation of women would do any better.

Peter adapted more easily. Most men did. They started new careers with new challenges. In those post-war years, servicewomen lacked the opportunities of today. It took me 60 years to learn that young RAF officers on demobilisation were offered the chance of a free university education. The men that is, not the women. I resolved I too would graduate one day.

I am sure that the circumstances that led to so many of us taking on responsibilities at such an early age made us more resilient. I know that it was these experiences that have marked my life until now. It gave me the strength and the courage to face the loss of Peter just as we retired, after we had worked together in the hotel industry for many years. It helped me to face the heartbreaking loss of my only son at the early age of fifty. It armed me with the determination to study for the university degree I had always wanted, and to achieve it at the age of eighty-seven! The war years forged the iron strength and resolution of so many of that generation, giving us the ability to search for any opportunity that life might present and the confidence and flexibility to grasp it with both hands.

Epilogue

Reminiscing

To search back into my memory of the wartime years has been a journey of nostalgia, of pride and of sadness. Nostalgia because of the friendships formed, the triumphs over disasters, the memories of challenges faced; pride at having contributed in some small way to the survival of my homeland, and sadness at the sufferings I have seen, the friends I have lost and the cruelty of fellow man.

After the war I kept the promise that I made when I signed the Official Secrets Act that I would not speak about the Filter Room for 30 years. This secrecy has meant that the vital work we did is still unknown and unappreciated.

In writing this book to set the record straight, I have stirred emotions which lay dormant for all that time. During my research I have traced some of those who shared with me those days and nights of excitement, of horror and of comradeship, and learned how they have faced their future with courage.

I have thought of those whom I met on the way – the young man who wrote the letter of goodbye, did he ever return? I thought of my first love, George, and wondered if he was remembered by those he saved from the beaches of Dunkirk. I have remembered the plotters and tellers, the Controllers, the Movement Liaison teams and the Filterer Officers who shared those long hours of duty with me; so many wonderful people who have coloured my life.

The pilots in their Spitfires and Hurricanes in The Battle of Britain will always be remembered in the history of our country.

Will the generations to come ever hear about or remember the small band of women who went to war and contributed to that victory in the Filter Rooms of RAF Fighter Command in the defence of Britain?

Postscript

For over seventy years, I wondered about the three French children, Francois, Jean and Hélène Boucher, to whom I taught English in 1938 and was forced to leave at the time of the Munich Crisis.

Through the Internet I learnt their father's story. Marcel Boucher, a highly-decorated World War One Officer, trained as a lawyer and became mayor of the spa resort Contrexeville. Although a politician, he also founded Les Compagnons de Jeanne d'Arc, a patriotic and religious organisation. Later he was elected a member of the French Parliament for the Vosges region. In 1940 when Germany occupied France, he joined the Vichy government of Marshal Pétain. With Allied victory imminent and fearing reprisals, he fled with his family to Germany in 1944, later taking refuge in Argentina.

Recently I made contact with Geneviève Moulard, a French writer. She offered to trace the Boucher children and within weeks she phoned to say she had found Hélène and had given her my telephone number. Within an hour Hélène, now seventy-nine, was speaking to me in impeccable English. This was her story.

The children were sent ahead to Germany, followed by their parents. In preparation, all available money was turned into jewellery, sewn in a bag and placed round Hélène's waist. She was unaware of its contents. She travelled with the German school she attended in France and joined the Hitler Jugend. She said she enjoyed it. It was so organised! In 1945 the family moved to Italy, obtaining Vatican approval. Hélène attended a convent school there. A year later, via Spain, they finally took refuge in Argentina, where he attempted to establish a series of spas, similar to Contrexeville.

The post-war French government accused Marcel Boucher of collaboration and confiscated all his property but in 1950, he returned to France to face his accusers. His lawyer successfully pleaded his innocence, maintaining his client was a committed anti-communist but never was pro-Hitler. Marcel's property was returned to him. He immediately sold everything and returned to Argentina. He died in 1968 during a visit to Montevideo, Uruguay where he had property. His wife survived him for twenty years.

Meanwhile, Francois, the elder boy, reluctantly trained as a civil engineer and fathered seven children with several wives. Becoming an ardent mountaineer in the Andes, he went on to earn his living making equipment for this sport. He died at the age of eighty. Jean graduated from the Lycée Francais in Buenos Aires. He spent a year in Canada learning hotel management but preferred to become a pharmaceutical representative, travelling throughout Argentina. Married to an Anglo-Argentinean, he had three children and later moved to Venezuela dying in 1995. Hélène was a boarder in an Irish convent in Buenos Aires, obtaining a Cambridge overseas certificate and later spent a year in a Californian college. On her return, like Francois no longer sharing her parents' social values, she felt confident to make her own way. Her father had insisted all the children learnt several foreign languages. Proficient in German, Spanish, Italian and English as well as French, she worked in Argentina and Tunisia, in a variety of posts, ranging from model to saleswoman then secretary. Above all she is proud to have been an air hostess for two years with S.A.S, as well as studying to become a surgical nurse. From her photos, she was a beautiful young woman. Finally settling in Switzerland, she was secretary to the Refugee Department of the World Council of Churches for seventeen years.

Now happily retired, she has made her home in Geneva. Her life, which promised so much in those sunny days of May 1938, has seen many changes but she is a survivor and I hope she has now found peace. Perhaps one day we will meet again.

GLOSSARY

AI	Radar for air interception
Arbeitsdienst	Compulsory German youth work service
Army Co-Op	Army Co-Operation aircraft
Aspirin	Allies aid against German Knickenbein
ATS	Auxiliary Territorial Service
ATA	Air Transport Auxiliary0
AWOL	Absent without leave
BIG BEN	Code name for V2 attacks
CH	Radar Chain Home equipment
CHEL	Radar Chain Extra Low equipment
CHL	Radar Chain Home Low equipment
CSD	Clerk special duties
CMP	Corps Military Police
Demob	Demobilisation to civilian life
DRO	Daily Routine Orders
Enigma	German coding machine
EVT	Educational and vocational training
FFI	Free from infection
Filterer	Officer, collating, correcting Radar information
Filter Officer	Officer supervising Filter Room activities
Filter Plotter	Filter room plotters of Radar information
GCI	Ground Controlled Interception
Gee	Radio navigational interception aid
Gen	General information
Gold braid	Officers of high rank
Goniometer	Instrument measuring elevation angle
Ground ray	Static responses of buildings etcetera
Headache	Knickelbein system to target bombing raids.
IFF	Identification friend or foe
Knickenbein	German bombing beams
KR	Movement liaison officer
Lord Haw Haw	American traitor, German propagandist
Luftwaffe	German Air Force
Ma'am	Customary address to WAAF Officers
MARU	Mobile Advance Reporting Unit
Mayday	SOS signal
Mess	Dining area for all HM Forces

MLO	Movements Liaison Officer
Mulberry Harbour	Artificial harbour used in D Day landings
NAAFI	Navy, Army and Air Force Institute
Oboe	Radio navigational aid to bombing target
OCTU	Officer Cadet Training Unit
Operation Bulldog	Navigation exercise for U S Army Air Force
Operation Crossbow	Operation against German V1 & V2 weapons
Operation Overlord	Allied landings in June 1944
Operation Sea Lion	Hitler's planned invasion of Britain
Ops Room	Operations room, either Group or Sector
Oswald	Radar device to record short trace of V2
Panzer Division	German tank division
Penguin	Nickname for RAF non-air crew
Petainiste	Supporter of pro-Nazi President Petain
PMC	President of Messing Committee
Polar diagram	Polar coordinates of angle of elevation
Put on a charge	Penalty for misdemeanour
Radar	Radio direction and ranging
RDF	Radio direction finding
Remuster	Change trade or branch
SHAEF	Supreme Headquarters Allied Expeditionary Force
Summerfield Tracking	Metal grid used to create temporary runway
TAF	Tactical Air Force
Teller	WAAF corporal relaying filtered information
u/s	Useless, invalid, out of order
WAAF	Women's Auxiliary Air Force
Wehrmacht	German Army
Wingless wonder	Similar to "penguin" non-aircrew
WRAF	Women's Royal Air Force, current name of WAAF
X raid	Unidentified or doubtful raid